MARILYN
INTIMATE EXPOSURES

MARILYN
INTIMATE
EXPOSURES

BY SUSAN BERNARD

Images by Hollywood's Great Glamour Photographer Bruno Bernard

Essays by Lindsay Lohan and Jane Russell

NORMA JEAN DOUGHERTY
alias Marilyn Monroe
in Bernard's Hollywood Studio (July 24, 1946)

STERLING
New York

STERLING
New York

An Imprint of Sterling Publishing
387 Park Avenue South
New York, NY 10016

ISBN 978-1-4027-8001-1

VERVE
EDITIONS

Production management by
Verve Editions for Sterling Publishing.

Design by
The Grillo Group, Inc. Chicago.

Distributed in Canada by
Sterling Publishing
c/o Canadian Manda Group
165 Dufferin Street
Toronto, Ontario, Canada M6K 3H6
Distributed in the United Kingdom by
GMC Distribution Services
Castle Place, 166 High Street
Lewes, East Sussex
England BN7 1XU
Distributed in Australia by
Capricorn Link (Australia) Pty. Ltd.
P.O. Box 704
Windsor, NSW 2756, Australia

For information about custom editions,
special sales, and premium and
corporate purchases, please contact
Sterling Special Sales at 800-805-5489
or specialsales@sterlingpublishing.com.

Printed in China

2 4 6 8 10 9 7 5 3 1

www.sterlingpublishing.com

For further information, please contact:
www.bernardofhollywood.com
Email: Keylighton@aol.com
Inquiries, Bernard of Hollywood Pub.
Los Angeles, CA, USA
Phone: (323) 935-0035
Please contact Susan Bernard's client
coordinator, Patricia Campbell

Photos © Renaissance Road, Inc.
Los Angeles

Text © Susan Bernard, Los Angeles

Photo Editorial by Susan Bernard
Los Angeles

Photo Credits
R. Dietrich—ullstein bild/The Granger
Collection. Pg. 11.
David Wills Collection. Pg. 89.
Photo Tom Kelley, Cartwright's
Calendar. Pg. 101.
Photographer unknown. Pg. 121.
David Wills Collection. Pg. 173.
Bettmann/CORBIS. Pg. 175.
Bettmann/CORBIS. Pg. 175.
AP Photo. Pg. 176.
SNAP/Rex USA. Pg. 177.
Bettmann/CORBIS. Pg. 178.
Joshua Miller. Pg.179.
Maurice Rinaldi. Pg. 197.

Pg. 70. expert from *Conversations with
Kafka* by Gustav Janouch, translated by
Goronwy Rees, from CONVERSATIONS
WITH KAFKA, copyright ©1968 by S.
Fischer Verlag GMBH, translation
copyright ©1971 S. Fischer Verlag
GMBH. Reprinted by permission of
New Directions Publishing Corp.

Pg. 98. "The Madness" from *Selected
Poems*, by Rainer Maria Rilke, translated
by C. F. MacIntyre. (c) 1968 by C. F.
MacIntyre. Published by the University
of California Press.

In memory of my mother and
best friend, Ruth Brande Bernard,
who graced our lives.

Author's mother Ruth Brande Bernard, circa 1950s.

CONTENTS

Opposite: Bruno Bernard, self-portrait, 1946.

Following pages: the Museum of Modern Art's *Fame After Photography* installation
of the sixty-foot high Marilyn in White on the Museum exterior, 1999.

LINDSAY LOHAN

Lindsay Lohan has been channeling Marilyn Monroe for years; she embodied the very essence of Marilyn for *New York Magazine's* 2008 photo session, recreating photographer Bert Sterns' iconic "The Last Sitting." Although terrified of stripping bare for the shoot, Lindsay agreed and said, "It's really an honor." Lindsay has been building a multimedia alter to Marilyn. The clothing line she created, 6126, is in homage to her patron saint's birthday. She humorously recreated my dad's signature photo of Marilyn with her skirt blowing over the subway grate in the 2011 spoof film "Underground Comedy"—her own pleated white skirt billowing, handguns cocked, targeting the paparazzi as if they were sitting ducks in a shooting gallery.

When Lindsay Lohan tattooed Marilyn's quote "Everyone's a star and deserves the right to twinkle," with yellow, blue, and green stars on her inner wrist, the sacred Lindsay-Marilyn pact was sealed. Now, I can't help but wonder if Marilyn has chosen to speak through Lindsay from wherever she is. I can see her long blonde tresses, once copper in tone, shaping her luminous features; hear that distinct throaty voice.

I was twelve and watching the film "Niagara" over and over again when I was shooting *The Parent Trap.* I didn't refer to it as *film noir* then. I just thought it was dark and full of emotion. Marilyn was the beautiful bad girl in that tight, rose-colored dress. The character she played was strong and taking control, which I unconsciously knew at that young age was a necessary quality for a woman. I had seen what my mother, whom I love, had gone through with my father. She, I and my brother Michael, my sister Aliana, and my youngest brother Dakota were in a constant state of uncertainty. I would have to put myself between him and my siblings.

I can understand the photographer Bernard of Hollywood's statement, "it took a superhuman effort to be Marilyn." I identify. Without any real family to come home to and no education, Marilyn managed to have her dream. The dream of a little girl looking out of an orphanage window at the RKO sign, and promising herself, "There must be thousands of girls sitting alone like me, dreaming of becoming a movie star. But I'm not going to worry about them. I'm dreaming the hardest."

People in their mind have created who I am and act as if there is no real person inside of me. Just like Marilyn, who created the blonde sex goddess on camera. But inside, she was this whole other person who had intellect, wrote poetry, and gave her all to mastering her art. Dreamed of being a mother one day. Marilyn once said it takes five hours to "become" Marilyn.

Marilyn never wanted to be just a celebrity. Neither do I. I started working in commercials, when I was three. I always wanted to be in great films. I had always thought that movie stars were in films that would last forever in your mind. But now the films don't. I don't want to be remembered as someone who just wanted to be photographed, who goes out at night, and gets in trouble. Look, I never had a normal high school life. I was homeschooled for two years, never had a high school prom or went to college. I was just sort of acting out that period of time I never had, and I made some bad choices. So all the tabloids, just like with Marilyn, keep harping on my mistakes. Heath Ledger once said to me, "It's build you up to knock you down and that's all it is. And you just have to see if you can stand through it."

"She's so young and she's so alone out there in the world in terms of structure and, you know, people to nurture her. And she's so talented." That's what I read Jane Fonda said about me after we filmed "Georgia Rule." Jane was right about no structure.

Marilyn said she had no foundation. But she said she was really working on it. I've been trying to do the same thing. But sometimes a relationship doesn't work out like you'd hoped. The tabloids don't give you a chance. They don't want to know who you are inside. If everything's OK with you, who wants to hear about it? I believe in myself and I'm a good actress. I've been lucky enough to work with some of the most respected actors and directors at a very young age.

It took time for Marilyn to be taken seriously as an actress. She risked everything and broke her contract with Fox studios, demanded more money, approval of directors, better scripts, more respect, and formed Marilyn Monroe Productions. That was really empowering for a woman in the '50s. Marilyn was not a victim. She took control. And we remember her, 50 years later, for her "great films."

—Lindsay Lohan

Lindsay Lohan, 2011.

JANE RUSSELL

Jane Russell was holding court in the summer of 2010 at the Playboy Mansion's Midsummer Night's Dream Party. She sat at the head of a long Mahogany dining table, a genuine Picasso lurking overhead, surrounded by those of Hollywood's new generation who flashed their cell phones, politely asking to be photographed with her, and by those who waited for an opening, a moment to sit down right beside her and chat, hoping to be touched, graced by a time and place in Hollywood that no longer exists. Jane laughed. Her wit was sharp and her eyebrows were on to perfection. She was excited to be celebrating her 90th birthday in London.

She was ageless and determined. She said, "Susan, I don't like phone interviews and if something happens, just go read my book, *Jane Russell: My Paths and My Detours*. I said everything I want to say about Marilyn in it." I told her nothing was going to happen, as I put my arm around her fragile shoulder camouflaged by a satin, violet gown. I asked her what she recalled and she replied without hesitation, "Marilyn was always asking me about Joe, Joe DiMaggio. She wanted to know what it would be like to be married to an athlete because I was married to one and I told her, 'You're going to get to know a lot of guys.'" She smiled. And then Jane went into a trance, shaking her head back and forth and playing with an empty glass with ice cubes. "Marilyn, oh Marilyn," she murmured to herself. "What happened? What happened to her?"

Marilyn had a great desire for knowledge and self-improvement. I told Marilyn that she must find time to go off with her own friends to talk about books and poetry and arts. But apparently she wasn't able to go off and do that. Marilyn felt a part of her was dying, she wasn't expressing herself when she was with Joe. I think if she had gone back with Joe, her life wouldn't have been so lonely, and her life wouldn't have ended the way it did.

She needed spiritual guidance. She had no higher power to count on, no foundation. Some of my friends and I started spiritual meetings in our homes for people in show business, who felt it was difficult going to a strange church. I talked Marilyn into coming to a meeting, but she didn't think it was for her.

Darryl Zanuck, the head of 20th Century Fox, had bought Gentlemen Prefer Blondes for Marilyn to star in. This was to be her first big picture. The director Howard Hawks wanted me to play

Dorothy, Lorelei's best friend. We started dance rehearsals with Jack Cole, and Gwen Verdon. Jack worked dancers to death, but with Marilyn and me, he was patience itself. She was determined that her bosses at Fox were going to take her seriously. Marilyn would stay for an hour or two after I left, and he'd stay with her. I had never seen any actor with such drive to rehearse; she did not allow herself to get tired. Me, I needed at least 10 hours of sleep. She didn't allow herself to be satisfied easily. Jack said she wouldn't really learn anymore during that time, but he understood her insecurity. We all refer to her as "Baby Doll."

Natasha Lytess, her drama coach, worked with her every night. Marilyn would come in the morning, way before me, and she'd be rehearsing with her again. Natasha began directing her right in front of Hawks. This became a big problem. Finally, Hawks threw Natasha off the set. After that, Marilyn often ran off to her dressing room crying.

Marilyn was always ready, but she could not make herself come out of her dressing room. You don't keep Howard Hawks waiting! Whitey, her make up man, confided in me that she was simply afraid to go out and face Hawks. Everyone was complaining, "Why isn't she coming out?" I would go to her dressing room and say, "Come on, 'Blondl'! It's five of. Let's go get them!" Marilyn would look up at me like a little girl, with those big, blue-grey eyes and say in child like voice, "Ok."

We got along great together. Marilyn was very shy and sweet, and far more intelligent that people gave her credit for. The press tried their best to work up a feud between us, but they were sniffing up the wrong tree.

Marilyn asked me how I found time to manage both a career in acting, and a home, and children. "It seemed impossible to me," Marilyn said. "When I go out at night," I explained, "I put the studio completely out of my mind. You've got to have a good housekeeper to run the house for you, and cook. Then when you come home, you have plenty of time to concentrate on your family. I know lots of women in Hollywood who are doing it Marilyn.

I was pleased with Marilyn's decision to move out of the Beverly Hills Hotel and into her own flat on Doheny Drive. I helped her organize it. I told her it will give you a nice feeling of security to be in your own home with your own furniture and things. You've got to get used to managing your own home before you get married to Joe. Every woman should have her own home. Hotel life is no kind of life for a woman.

I believe that the outstanding quality that made Marilyn different from the other so-called sex symbols was her vulnerability. Everyone wanted to take care of her, to help. She brought out protectiveness in all but the insensitive, or those who, of course, simply wanted a more sophisticated adult world where everyone was responsible to himself, a world of caustic humor, a take-as-much-as-you-give world. I was accustomed to that world, but Marilyn could get terribly hurt. She simply could not understand people being mean. She was super sensitive and with good reason, considering her rudderless and unsure future.

I remember it was beach time again for my family and the days were long and wonderful. When the guys were hunting, or at training camp, my girlfriends, and sisters-in-law, and their kids were there. We all helped, so there was loads of leisure time. We philosophized, laughed at our problems and giggled, and the kids had a ball because they had their friends.

At night we showered, put on caftans, had wine, music, and more talk by the fire. If the others went to bed, I often sat and stared at the water "night dreaming." One lone boat was lit up all the way

out on the horizon and spots of light from the house lit the waves as they endlessly rolled in. A time alone at night was always necessary to me during those people filled years.

On one such a night, I thought of Marilyn Monroe. I wished I had her phone number, because I knew she belonged there, where we were all laughing about our problems.

The next day, my husband Robert arrived from a hunting trip and said, "Marilyn Monroe's dead, I heard it on the radio." We were all stunned. If only, if only . . .

Over 50 years ago, Marilyn told me, "If they aren't going to be fair and nice, I can always leave." She left, but on the screen and in Bruno's photographs, we are reminded of her sweetness, humor and how she glowed.

—Jane Russell

Jane Russell, circa 1950.

INTRODUCTION

By Susan Bernard

"It's clear that Bernard had a totally original eye. He was not making standard Hollywood glamour photos. They're not George Hurrell-style portraits, which often seem to carry a symbolic, abstract quality, where they're almost like sculpture. Bernard had a way of making his subjects seem more human. When you see his pictures—whether it's Sonja Henie at the Racquet Club or Bing Crosby at Ciro's—you want to stop and look at them, because of the obvious connection between the subject and the camera. Bernard's work just has more information, more texture, more meat."

—Carol Kismaric, Curator, the Museum of Modern Art, New York, *Fame After Photography* Exhibition.

In 1999, I gazed up at the skyscrapers of New York City set against a gray-blue sky and there she was—Dad's Marilyn, sixty feet tall on the exterior of the Museum of Modern Art, floating as if reaching for a boundless universe, her white halter dress tied in a bow behind her neck, dress billowing from side to side as if angel wings, just as Truman Capote once put it, "the dream of being able to fly." She is unabashedly blissful. Her transparent white panties revealing she is not blonde all over.

As I stood there in the sweltering heat of that July afternoon, I thought of the relevance of his photograph of Marilyn nearly fifty years later. He recorded and idolized the post World War II working-class woman who dared to step out of the kitchen.

I recalled another image from the same photographic session in which she is holding down her white skirt, her expression is one of pleasure. She is both satisfying the Puritanism of 1950's American and mocking it. Housewives, secretaries, shop girls—decades before Women's Liberation—would see Marilyn's life and view their own with new eyes.

My mind races to 1937, to a young man of twenty-seven, a German Jewish immigrant. Tears are veiling his eyes as he clutches the ocean liner's rail. He is oblivious to the bitter wind crossing his water-stained cheeks. In the distance, he sees the shores of America, the towering magnificence of the Statue of Liberty. She promises, you will no longer be alone and penniless. You have fled to America, the land of the free, with only the used Rolleiflex box camera your mother, Sophia, had given you in the Auerbach orphanage, when you were eleven. You are a survivor to the core. Embrace the American Dream. You endured the tortures of Nazism, the loss of your homeland, your family and loved ones. You drove with a vengeance in the midst of fear and chaos to obtain a doctorate in criminal law from the University of Kiel, a privilege granted to only one percent of young Jews, "I will fight for the underdog, the poor, the forgotten," you swore. A month later, the Nuremberg Laws forbade Jews to practice law.

As a leader in an underground Jewish youth organization, you negotiated the release of thousands of Jews to Palestine. You were on the Gestapo list, facing the door of death. You will never forget on the eve of your historic escape to Rio de Janeiro, hiding, sitting at the Ufa Palace cinema house. You will never forget being moved by the camaraderie between Clark Gable and Spencer Tracy in the film, *San Francisco,* as they faced earthquake and fire. A skyline magenta, pumpkin, golden, a flame, bodies thrown about, piled, buried. Smoke rising. You will never forget changing your destination to California. You completed your studies at Berkeley. You will never forget the smoke filled Anhalt train platform, where your frail mother made a super human effort to run with the train, to catch one more glimpse of her son, with her one half-good eye. You will never forget how she ran shouting, "Take care of yourself, my boy." And so it shall be written that this would be the last time that you would ever see her sweet face.

Marilyn and my father were survivors to the core.

Torn between academics and the arts and having completed his post-graduate studies at Berkeley, Dad changed the course of his life once more moving to Hollywood and becoming a director's apprentice to Max Reinhardt, the magician of German theater. Unable to get into the Directors Union, he earned money photographing the children of the Hollywood elite. Despite obscurity and lack of funds, he set up his first darkroom in the basement of his Hollywood apartment in 1940. Shortly thereafter, he moved his studio to the famous Sunset Strip. "No one knew the name Bernard, but they all knew Hollywood," my dad declared and created his trademark signature, Bernard of Hollywood, that for decades captured the image of glamour.

Dad has been called the "Rembrandt of Glamour Photography" and the "Vargas of the Pin-Up." Of all the accolades that have been bestowed upon him, the one that gave him the most joy

Party for Marilyn, Los Angeles, 1953.

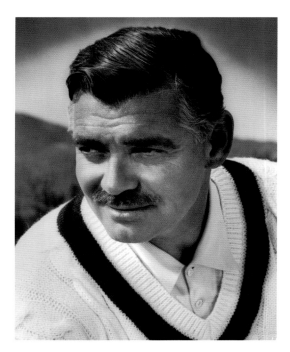

New York columnist Walter Winchell saw this photograph of Clark Gable and crowned Dad the "Rembrandt of Photography," 1952.

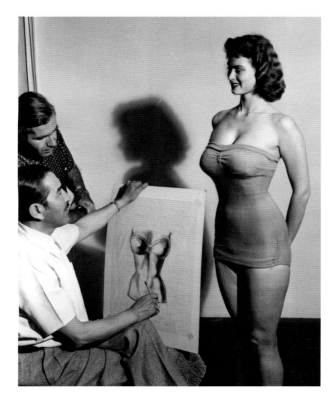

Bruno Bernard and mentor, illustrator Alberto Vargas, at work with actress Irish McCalla, 1949.

was "the man who discovered Marilyn Monroe." He took great pride in his ability to uncover in Norma Jean the mysterious photogenic qualities that transformed a nice-looking girl into a larger-than-life, illusionary beauty. Glamour photography has been described as "making a silk purse out of a sow's ear." However, had it not been for her almost pathological obsession with becoming a star, coupled with her uncanny ability to transform herself before the camera, Norma Jean would not have become Marilyn and stepped onto the illustrious stage of the goddesses' pantheon.

Marilyn's sexuality landed during America's optimistic 50s— a time of affluence and renewed beliefs and fears. In the fifth grade, I'd duck under my desk table, nuclear destruction, our teacher warned, was imminent. Then came communism and male anxiety on the heels of the sexual revolution, heralded by *Playboy* publishing Marilyn as Miss December 1953. Hugh Hefner sold his apartment furniture and for $500, purchased the rights to a nude photo of Norma Jean, which appeared on a Brown & Bigelow calendar he spotted in a mechanic's garage. She was his first "girl next door" in the centerfold. Broke, she had posed for the calendar. Hefner dreamed of creating the American male's fantasy in a magazine. Over 50 years later, he attributes his empire to the success of that premier issue and to his golden girl, Marilyn Monroe. They would never meet.

In scanning Marilyn's life, through endless photographs and Dad's written word, I, like many women, identify with her. Our vulnerabilities, aspirations and dodging of what haunts us are the evident parallels. My father also discovered me at the tender age of seventeen, just as he discovered Norma Jean 1946. In 1965 by chance, I accompanied him to Chicago where he was to have an editorial meeting at *Playboy* magazine. Just like Marilyn over a decade before, I chose to not be ashamed of my femininity and empower myself, long before the emancipation promised by Women's Liberation. and consequently I became Miss December 1966. And like Marilyn, who took risks, I believed that a woman could be intelligent and still be desirable and make dreams come true, just as men did. Subsequently, in my early 20s, I was both an actress and the head of my own film and television production company. Similar to Marilyn, I also was separated on-and-off from the love of my life, Jason Miller, yet we maintained a deep affinity for one another, just like Marilyn and Joe DiMaggio. Ironically, Marilyn's second husband, like mine, was a Pulitzer Prize-winning playwright with the same last name—Miller.

Sadly, Marilyn had no family. My mother was my best friend, and I doted on Dad. I had the child Marilyn longed for. What if I hadn't had this basic foundation? Would I have drowned in the Hollywood well, unable to swim up? I now better understand Dad's state-ment, "It took superhuman efforts to be Marilyn Monroe." Marilyn told my dad bluntly,

> I love to do things the censors won't pass. Both the anti-commu-nists on the House Un-American Activities Committee and the movie censors on the Production Board should be buried alive.

The mythology of Marilyn has inspired, taunted and mystified countless lives. Her image is more alive today—50 years after her passing—than in her lifetime. And as the mythology is perpetuated in the world by admirers, historians and writers, who make it up as they go along; filmmakers, ex-husbands and photographers, who each think they have captured the "real" Marilyn; and biographers, who find angles, but never find the real thing: they weave fantastic scenarios surrounding her death, they all share a secret, they all were her "close friends."

She stays in our consciousness, teetering on invented history and memory. She haunts me with many questions that will never be answered, but what comes back to me are my father's photographs of her. This truth I protect.

Since Dad's passing in 1987, I founded Bernard of Hollywood Publishing, which preserves, exhibits and publishes his photographic legacy. What is astonishing is that I was also taking on Marilyn's legacy and she belongs to everyone. As Diane Arbus' daughter Amy expressed to me, "A blessing and a curse."

To me, Marilyn is an intangible angel. She is part of the family. Where I go, she follows. And when I fall, she is there to pick me up. Being part of the mythology of Marilyn has produced battles beyond my wildest expectations. I have walked up the stairs of the New York Federal Court to defend her and my Dad's photographic rights, and I won.

The photos turn up like bad pennies and turn to gold. Twenty-five thousand photographs were discovered in a cellar in Hamburg, Germany. They cross oceans and arrive at my front door without signatures from defunct photo agencies, show up at fine art galleries, get into the hands of the nameless who sit in coffee shops and sell them for a dime, race like greyhounds online. They are duplicated, altered, and yet always find their way back to where they belong.

In compiling this book, I began again tracing Marilyn and my Dad's history, sifting through archival numbered boxes stacked in chronological order, capturing crucial moments of her life. Boxes filled with copyright-stamped 8-x-10's with typed descriptions taped on their backs, original and duplicate negatives, internegs, transparencies, slides, proofs, contact sheets, hiding in yellowing photo sleeves with my Dad's scratched notes. Always searching for the "big find," the undiscovered image, yet willing to settle for a great, unpublished outtake, a revelation in his notes. Perusing online with my right hand, Patricia, photo agencies licensing thousands of Marilyn images, searching and finding illegal usages. Rummaging through suitcases piled to the ceiling, unopened, packed with dusty European magazines and newspapers, underlined Xeroxed articles, typed onion skin papers and illegible handwritten notes in German, with the thought I would discover a better understanding of why, toward the end of my Dad's life, while battling cancer and imminent death, he was obsessed with

the conspiracy stories surrounding Marilyn's death. He wrote to Robert Kennedy's lawyer, John Bates, as though Marilyn were "the underdog, the poor, the forgotten." He was defending Marilyn, who could not defend herself. As my dad made clear,

> On the basis of my longtime personal acquaintance with Marilyn and my critical analysis of some of the second-generation witnesses, I have dismissed the murder plot perpetrated by either the Kennedys, the mafia, or the CIA agents as pure sensationalist speculations.

> If I do not finish this, my daughter, Susan Bernard, will finish my life's work for me.

On a psychological level, he untangled the theories, lined up the suicide attempts, counted the miscarriages, listed the numerable prescription drugs inhaled, included her mother in a Norwalk, California insane asylum and the grandmother who had died there, the marriages that had failed, and he concluded,

> Norma Jean killed Marilyn in installments.

> More specifically, the better half of her, Norma Jean, who could not bear to live together with the monster Marilyn any longer. The correct psychological diagnosis that cuts far deeper than the coroner's knife lays bare the roots of this type of self-destruction. Her lifelong endeavors to become a star at the expense of all other human emotions had made a vice out of a virtue. Her voluntarily posing in the nude in her last unfinished picture with the ominous title, *Something's Got to Give,* was symbolic. It was the vicious circle, to her way of thinking. At the zenith of her fame, she finished exactly as she had started, as a nude pin-up and because after all her valiant, almost super-human efforts, to break the mold of a sex symbol imposed upon her by the studio dictators, she submerged into it deeper than ever. After Marilyn surfaced momentarily out of the morass of glitter and glory, Norma Jean dragged her down for good.

Marilyn, Joe DiMaggio, and columnist Walter Winchell,
at Cinemascope first anniversary, 1954.

Marilyn and Dad both lived on the edge of hell toward the end. The demons of their tragic histories had caught up with them and they drove my dad's obsession. This is my understanding of the osmosis between two artists. Dad carefully orchestrated his final intentions in a state of unresolved torment and depression—not coincidentally, in the same way his beloved Marilyn had decades earlier. In his journal he wrote,

> Her death on this particular date was accidental rather than intentional. When through some unfortunate communication gaps in her last frantic calls for help no rescue came in time, she anesthetized her torment with more of a blend overdose of Nembutal sleeping pills and alcohol.

In the thick stack of his unfinished writings, I discovered evidence confirming my theory on the parallels between their lives.

My mission in this volume is to record the metamorphosis of Norma Jean to Marilyn and to document my dad's images that remain in our consciousness, forever frozen in time. The literal meaning of the word photographer, according to its Greek origin, is "light writer." I trust with camera and pen this pictorial essay celebrates with the light of compassion, the 50 years of Marilyn's enduring allure.

Opposite: Landmark Bernard of Hollywood photography studio on Sunset Boulevard, photograph of Gregory Peck in the window, 1947.

Above: A visitor before the silkscreen prints by Andy Warhol of Elizabeth Taylor, Marilyn Monroe and Jackie Kennedy. Across the room he sits, transfixed by Marilyn alone. Munich, 1982.

EULOGY: AUGUST 4, 1962

On August 5, 1962, the news of Marilyn Monroe's death escalated around the world. Dad heard it over the radio in Berlin, as he was having lunch in the rooftop restaurant of the Funkturm. A lump formed in his throat and he told the waiter to take away his half-eaten meal and bring him a cup of coffee. His mind raced back over space and time to Marilyn's first sitting, her whispery child-woman voice—"Mr. Bernard, can you take a few sexy pictures of me?"—echoing in his ears. He expressed how he felt a deep sense of shock. He was upset, since he was unable to help her when she needed him most. He grieved over the loss of the child-woman who was his "little sis." He fantasized how he would have rushed her to the hospital, where her stomach would have been pumped in time, and how he would have brought her back to the living. I imagine the news being broadcast continuously over the radio in the restaurant through a loudspeaker as Dad felt private pain and saw the impact of the tragic news on the saddened faces of the Berliners. To voice his grief, he immediately called his friend, the editor-in-chief of the *Berliner Illustriete Zeitung,* and told him to hold the presses for his eulogy. Half an hour later, in his pension, he dictated an article entitled "Goodbye Marilyn."

. . . Norma Jean/Marilyn, on your crypt we shall not jot down your vital statistics, 37-22-35, as you once suggested in one of your self-deprecating Norma Jean moods. Instead, we will mentally engrave the immortal verse of Goethe, a lifelong admirer of feminine beauty, that reads like poetic prophesy:

> *Distance does not make you complex*
> *you come flying out of breath*
> *to the light that in the end*
> *burns you, butterfly, to death.*

Now, over 50 years after Marilyn's passing and decades after Dad's, I can visualize him on that afternoon in August, walking the streets of Berlin, heading toward the international newsstand, finding his famous photo of her in white beneath the headlines of her passing—"Marilyn Monroe Muerta En 36," "Marilyn Monroe Retrouvée Morte," "마릴린 먼로는 자체 살인," "Мэрилин Мертвого," "Marilyn Si Suicida," quickly paying for the papers, hiding his anguish, disbelieving the reality in his hands.

Collage design by Bruno Bernard, 1984.

MARILYN MONROE
1926 — 1962

"Remember Bernie,
everything started with you!"
Marilyn Monroe

to Bruno Bernard in September, 1954

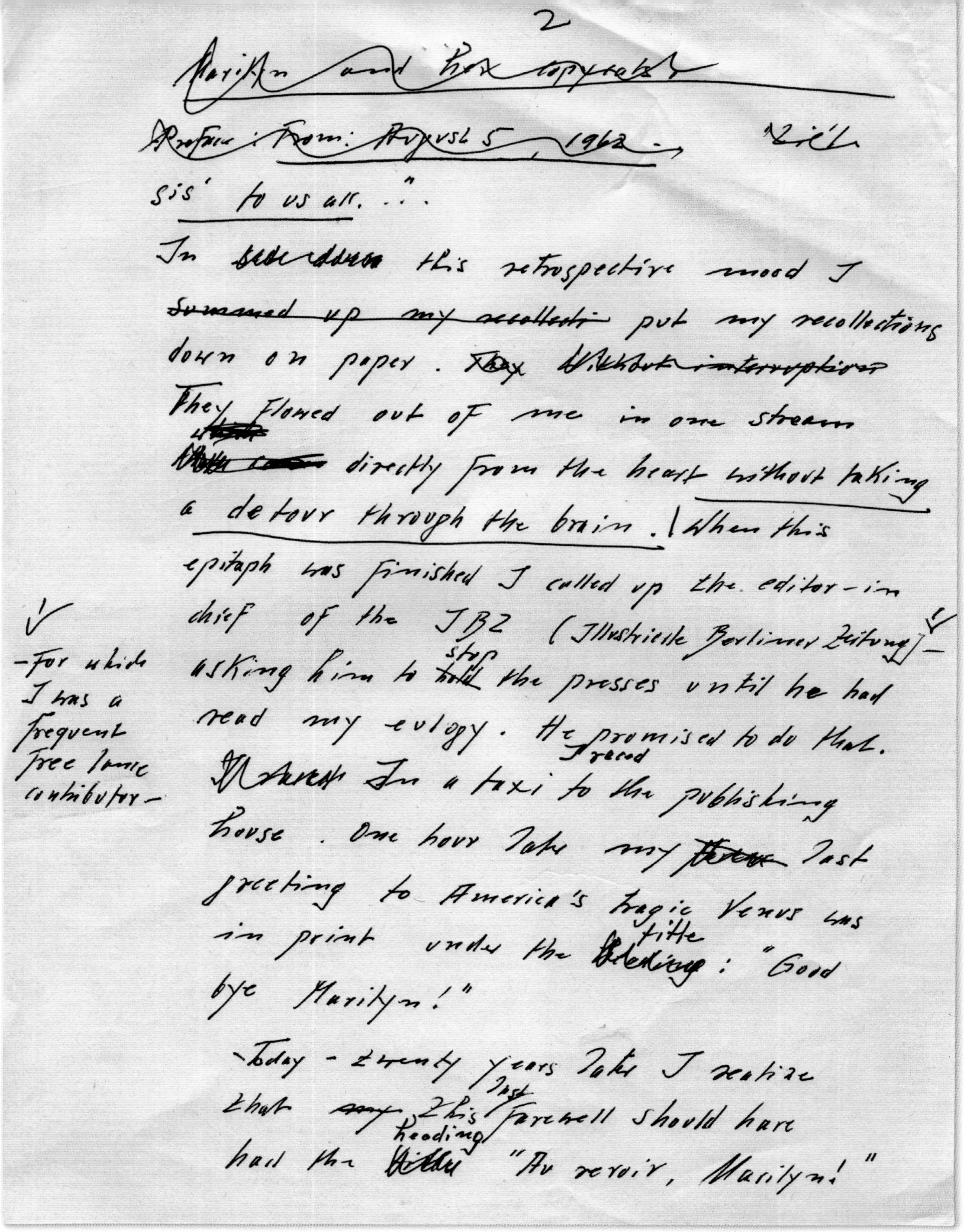

2

Marilyn and ~~Fox copyright~~

~~Preface: From:~~ August 5, 1962 — "Niet-
sis' to us all. . ."

In ~~his address~~ this retrospective mood I
~~summed up my recollecti~~ put my recollections
down on paper. ~~They without interruptions~~
They flowed out of me in one stream
~~without~~ directly from the heart without taking
a detour through the brain. | When this
epitaph was finished I called up the editor-in-
chief of the IBZ (Illustrierte Berliner Zeitung)
                                                    stop
asking him to ~~hold~~ the presses until he had
read my eulogy. He promised to do that.
                                    raced
~~I raced~~ In a taxi to the publishing
house. One hour late my ~~three~~ last
greeting to America's tragic Venus was
in print under the ~~heading~~ title: "Good
bye Marilyn!"

- For which
I was a
frequent
free lance
contributor —

- Today — twenty years late I realize
                                    last
that ~~my~~ this farewell should have
                    heading
had the ~~title~~ "Au revoir, Marilyn!"

Above: Bruno Bernard journal entry, 1962.

Opposite: Norma Jean, 1946.

CHAPTER 1

IN WHITE NEW YORK, 1954

Sept. 14, 1954. A very humid day in New York. What kind of life is it that starts with getting up at six o' clock in the morning in this asphalt jungle? Had I not accepted the *Redbook* assignment, and it wasn't with Marilyn, not ten horses could have drawn me from my Hollywood oasis to photograph *The Seven Year Itch* on its original location.

BRUNO BERNARD

In New York, Marilyn walks out of the Trans-Lux Theatre onto the movie set like a shaven lamb. She is peroxided, irritated, and raw; she is oblivious to the crowds multiplying on Lexington Avenue. She steps directly over the subway grate, moving four steps to the left, and comes down hard on heels, with the stance of a lion.

She is in her white sundress, with a halter-top gathered in folds accentuating real breasts. Legs are spread apart, feet in high-heeled white sandals. Her skirt is in the air, a billowing soft sheet, revealing fleshy thighs and transparent white cotton panties.

An exasperated director, Billy Wilder, holds up his megaphone, shouts, "Roll it!" for the sixteenth time. She throws her blonde head back, closing eyes in exhilaration, enjoying the warm breeze. She whispers, "Ahhh, what a relief?! Isn't it delicious?"

Marilyn Monroe on the New York set of *The Seven Year Itch*, 1954.

of Henry
Steig
HENRY STEIG
HATS
UME JEWELRY
Bernard of Hollywood

The crowds are silent. She is giving them what they want. She is not going to let them down.

A soundman picks up the ticking of a camera's metal motor drive. Wilder hollers, "Cut!"

Whitey, her makeup man, appears on the set, dabbing her nose and cleavage. She cherishes how he blushes when he calms her down, talks about his wife and kids.

She used to spend holidays with them when she had nowhere to go, when she used to pretend her mother was dead and the baby she had at thirteen was not hers. Now she has Joe.

Wilder stomps onto the set. "Say your lines slow. Distinct!" he directs her. Accentuating words, hands in the air, as if conducting a symphony.

She stares at him vacantly. The blue in her eyes has evaporated. "Let the skirt slowly lift," he tells her, as if she doesn't speak any English.

"She's fine!" he orders Whitey, " We're losing light."

"Take your time, honey," she tells Whitey.

Whitey is bringing his eye-level chair onto the set. Wilder throws his cap to the ground, spits on a monogrammed handkerchief, wipes his brow. She knows Wilder views her as a vacuum with erect nipples. She is circumventing the great Wilder. She's no *gag*.

Slowly Whitey is twisting a charcoal pencil on her cheek. Her head is tilted up, lids closed.

Her mind is wandering to the daughter she shall have. They are moving slowly along the Santa Monica pier, licking strawberry ice creams. Her daughter's rust hair flies in the sea wind. Eight and untouched.

Whitey gently adjusts her earrings, whispers, " Let's make this take a good one. We both want to fly this coop."

She harnesses her heels. Wilder shouts, "Roll it!"

Cool air is on bare calves. Eyes long to be a child and play. A slow wind lifts her hemline. She bends forward, the breeze crawls to thighs. Brazenly, she winks at the special effects man in a yellow construction hat under the subway grate, enjoying his manufactured wind machine and the wet pleasure it's bringing.

Marilyn Monroe and co-star Tom Ewell on the set of *The Seven Year Itch*, New York, 1954.

The skirt lifts. She teases the crowd, holding her skirt down with her hands. The sides of her skirt fly up: a patron saint, in the image of an angel bearing wings.

She is closing her eyes, opening them slightly. She sees Dad in the crowd. Was it really Bernie? She is snapping, zooming out of focus. She must be imagining it. The studio doctor's pills and injections to stop her hunger, insomnia, and escalating nerves.

Dad is positioning himself to her right, stooping to get an upward angle to elongate her legs. She is Norma Jean again. Eighteen. Her baby is breathing. Or is it the beat of her rapid pulse?

Why would Bernie be in New York? He records laced pink corsets, fishnet legs, sequined pasties in Vegas and Hollywood. He doesn't wait on movie sets. Perhaps the photographer has Bernie's same erudite manner and appeal. Did the photographer's little girl have bangs and auburn hair? Did she have dark colored hair? She couldn't remember. Had she simply taken too many pills? She couldn't recall.

She opens her eyes wide and it *is* him.

Wilder shouts, "Cut!" for the eighteenth time.

Like a child's pale pink petticoat, unabashedly flashing waist-high panties, the skirt lifts wildly. Face is completely covered. The machine is blowing stronger. She hears the crowds cheering louder.

Camera bulbs burst, like the shattering of glass.

Wilder repeats, roars, "Cut! Cut!"

She removes herself from the set, embraces Dad.

Wilder groans, 'The bitch."

Eyeliner streaks.

Wilder notices, wonders, "What the hell is he doing here? Bernard's never been a photographer for hire. She doesn't need another babysitter."

"What are you doing here?" she asks Dad in her breathless voice.

And for all within earshot to hear, she says to him, "Remember, Bernie. Everything started with you."

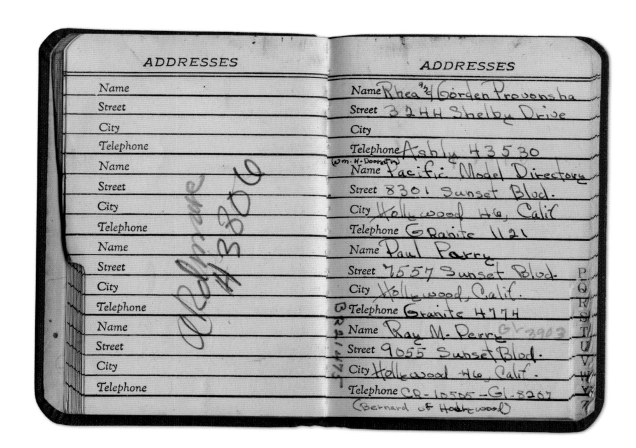

A page from the original 1946 Marilyn Monroe phone book with Bernard of Hollywood studio address and phone number handwritten by Norma Jean.

It was an emotional bond that Marilyn had to her public, the ordinary people, the guys in uniform—the working class, those who struggled through wars and the Depression, whose poverty was no shame—that drove Marilyn. They were her public and, like myself, she would never let them down.

BRUNO BERNARD

Marilyn Monroe on the set of *The Seven Year Itch*, New York, 1954.

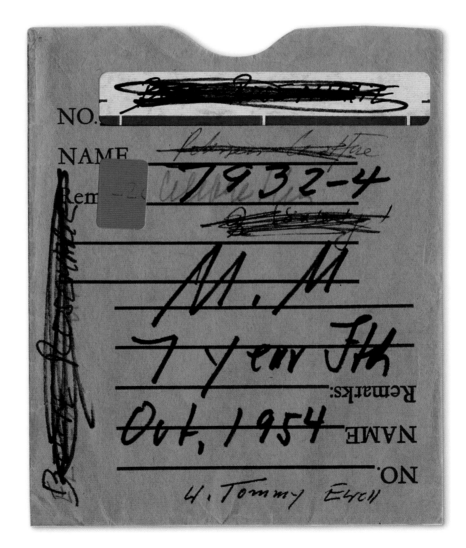

Opposite: Original contact sheet, *The Seven Year Itch*, 1954.

Top: Original black-and-white negative, 1954.

Bottom: Original negative sleeve, 1954.

The scene was repeated thirty times; Marilyn was fluffing her lines.

She wore only slightly transparent white silk panties under the

skirt. To the bystanders, it was evident that she was not blonde all

over. I refuse to retouch my photos. Joe DiMaggio, standing next to

Walter Winchell, was watching the exhibition directly across from me.

I could see DiMaggio's embarrassment turning to anger. Quickly,

I edged my way across the crowd, hoping to calm him down.

BRUNO BERNARD

Above: Original contact sheet, 1954.

Opposite: Marilyn's husband, baseball hero Joe DiMaggio, and New York columnist
Walter Winchell on the set of *The Seven Year Itch*, 1954.

"This is a little kid who wants to be with the other little kids sucking lollipops and watching the roller coaster, but can't because they won't let her. She's frightened to death of that public, which thinks she is so sexy. My God, if they only knew."

ALLEN "WHITEY" SNYDER, MAKEUP ARTIST

Marilyn with friend and makeup artist Allen "Whitey" Snyder, 1954. Whitey was Marilyn's close friend throughout her career. He was thrilled when I gave him this 11 x 14-inch color print in 1993. He had never possessed a color photograph of her with him.

Here and following pages:
Marilyn and co-star Tom Ewell, 1954.

"When you got her to the studio on a good day, she was remarkable. She had a quality that no one else ever had on the screen except Garbo. No one. She was a kind of real image beyond mere photography. She looked on the screen as if you could reach out and touch her."

BILLY WILDER

When the exasperated Wilder again began explaining the simplicity of the scene, Marilyn discovered me and winked me over, embracing me spontaneously. 'Bernie, what are you doing here?' she asked in her famous breathless whisper. And then she added, so the whole crew within earshot could hear, "Remember, Bernie. Everything started with you."

BRUNO BERNARD

Above: Marilyn, co-star Tom Ewell and director Billy Wilder on the New York set in front of the Trans-Lux Theatre, 1954.

Opposite: Director Billy Wilder and Marilyn, 1954.

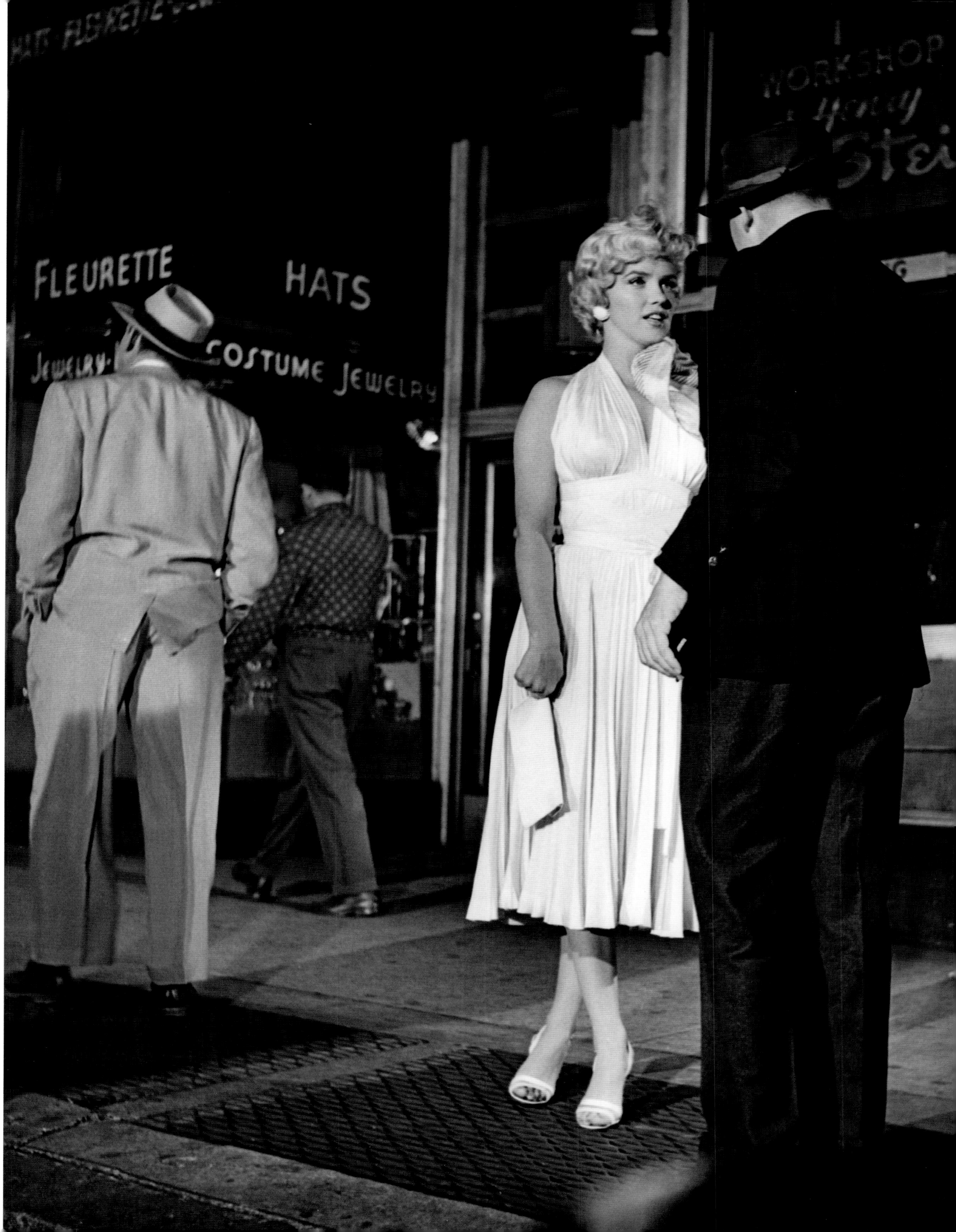
FLEURETTE
HATS
JEWELRY
COSTUME JEWELRY
WORKSHOP

The Yankee clipper attempted to cool off his Italian macho temper at Toot's Shor. Marilyn had continued giving her director and her ecstatic public their pound of flesh.

"I'll show Twentieth who Marilyn really is!" she told me, while Whitey powdered her cheek. "I'm going to form Marilyn Monroe Productions."

"Have you discussed this with Joe?"

"No, not yet. He just wants me to be a homemaker. He's the one that's embarrassed by the abuse Twentieth is giving me. Big breasts, big ass, big deal. I've had it!!"

This was the beginning of her perpetual search for glory, to satisfy her neurotic ambition; she was inflicting suffering upon both her professional and personal life, enjoying a vindictive triumph over the neglect of the unwanted and unloved child, Norma Jean.

BRUNO BERNARD

Marilyn and acting coach Natasha Lytess, 1954.

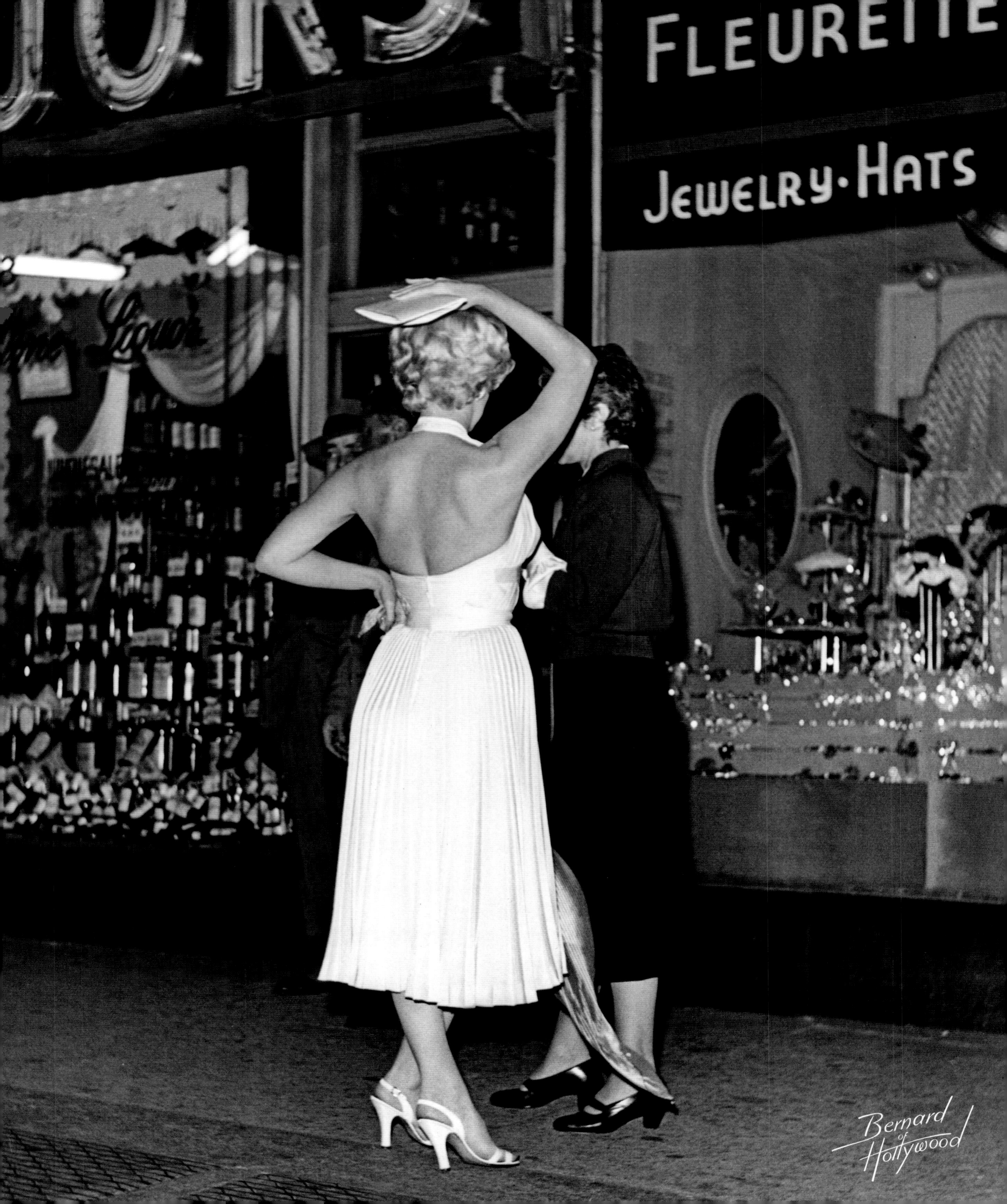
FLEURETTE
JEWELRY·HATS
Bernard of Hollywood

In 1993, I met the legendary director Billy Wilder.

"Thank you for meeting me," I said. His handshake was sturdy and compact.

I presented him with "Marilyn in White," 11 x 14-inches, artist-signed, double-matted, once printed in 1954 with noxious chemicals on Ektacolor, a paper no longer made. It is more apparent in an original photograph than an image on the back cover of my book that my dad didn't airbrush; darkness wasn't burned out in the developing. Time was smudging the artist's signature.

Wilder reached into his desk, just as I thought he would, put on another pair of glasses and appeared melancholy, his white eyebrows arched in a "V" like a gentle Santa Claus.

"She could deliver comedy better than anyone," he mumbled to himself.

Wilder took it back. "She was much better on screen than in person. New York acting lessons," he said, his eyes glued to the image. "She should have gone to train engineering school; then she would have known how to come on schedule."

Above: Matted print given to Billy Wilder, 1993.

Following pages: Studio screening room, 1954.

"It makes something in me happy to be late. People are waiting for me. People are eager to see me. I remember all the years I was unwanted, all the hundreds of times nobody wanted to see the little servant girl, Norma Jean— not even her mother. And I feel a queer satisfaction in punishing the people who are wanting me now. But it's not them I'm really punishing. It's the long-ago people who didn't want Norma Jean. The later I am, the happier she grows. To me, it's remarkable that I can get there at all."

MARILYN MONROE

CHAPTER 2

NORMA JEAN DOUGHERTY 1946–1948

"The best friend that these girls had, next to a diamond, was a glamour photographer'"

BRUNO BERNARD

Timing is everything. Or was it destiny? Perhaps it was something magical that, in July of 1946, brought the unknown Norma Jean Dougherty to walk aimlessly past my dad on Sunset Boulevard, just as he was leaving his dentist's office. And for him to follow her, give her his card and say, "Miss, this is strictly professional. I'd like to take some photo tests of you."

Norma Jean discovery series, first professional studio sitting, 1946.

Bernard
of
Hollywood

Bernard of Hollywood

PORTRAITS - PUBLICITY
9055 SUNSET BLVD.
HOLLYWOOD 46, CALIF.
PHONE: CR. 1-0505

365 S. COAST BLVD.
LAGUNA BEACH, CALIF.
PHONE: 4343

1 0 6 P L A Z A
PALM SPRINGS, CALIF.
PHONE: 7151

Release: 7/24/46

I hereby permit Bernard of Hollywood to use the pictures he has taken of me for exhibition and commercial use.

Signature:

Norma Jeane Dougherty

Hollywood was the flame to the moth. Every girl—the hometown cheerleader, the girl who was told by her boyfriend "You should be in pictures, dear"—rushed to Hollywood, crossing oceans, mountain ranges and deserts, on buses and trains, waiting at truck stops. Anyone could do this. You didn't have to be born a princess or go to Vassar. They came to sit at the right soda fountain. To get through the right door, meet the right person, the one that would reshape their destiny with a single phone call. They'd bleach their hair, wondering if it was blonde enough, buy new teeth, erase an accent, and commit fraud with a new name. Step up! Spin the wheel. Anyone can get lucky.

In this heated carnival of pink, frosted cotton candy and fast roller coasters, the talent scouts perused the fresh faces on the covers of men's magazines. If you had a good photo book, you'd be seen. It was part of the job to see newcomers. The studios had their own singing, dancing and acting schools. You could become part of the "groomed for stardom" factory, put under contract and even get a weekly check.

A Bernard of Hollywood photograph of a pretty girl with a twinkle in her eye in a two-piece polka dot or leopard print bathing suit accentuating cleavage in the post-war climate had become ubiquitous. His famous signature appeared on billboards, calendars and dozens of popular men's magazines. She was not only spinning the heads of the male species, she was also turning the wheels of commerce. She sold everything from socks to soap to sports cars, chocolates to girdles. She brought with her optimism, progress and a cash register Marilyn poignantly expressed,

> When I was eight I used to look out of the orphan asylum at night and see a big lighted up sign that read RKO Pictures. There must be thousands of girls sitting alone like me dreaming of becoming a movie star. But I am not going to worry about them. I'm dreaming the hardest.

At 6 a.m. sharp, Norma Jean's black Ford jalopy screeched to a halt outside 9055 Sunset Boulevard. The palm trees glistened and swayed. The sky was cobalt blue. She stood in front of the studio. Overwhelmed with wishes and expectations, she stared up at Dad's inviting Bernard of Hollywood signature above a life-size photo of Gregory Peck. The air was swept clean.

When she stepped into the reception room wearing heels a size too big, she sighed and asked, "Gee, do you really think I can make it as a cover girl model, Mr. Bernard?" He analyzed her schoolgirl face, which just like "Jeannie with the light brown hair," was framed with curls, and her complexion, which made her a walking advertisement for Ivory soap. He gazed at her figure, the kind G.I. Joes termed "built like a brick" and simply said, "Darling, my camera never lies." The glow in her heart was ignited and she believed anything was possible.

For Dad and Norma Jean, this time would remain in memory as an intangible bond of friendship that would outlast her marriages and various relationships with other men. Neither could have foreseen that the moment would become Hollywood history.

Opposite: Norma Jean Dougherty model release, 1946.

Above: Original negative, Norma Jean, 1946.

The Indian summer temperature had made the thermometer climb up over 90 degrees. After over two hours under the laser light of my dentist, I groggily left the office with a swollen cheek and slowly made my way back to my studio a few blocks away. While I was making up my mind whether to cancel my next appointment a dazzling teenager with a voluptuous figure wiggled by. She had curves in all the right places and she moved with the unadulterated movements of Lili St. Cyr and Tempest Storm when they were stripping on the stage of the Burbank Theater on Main Street. Could this be a nymphet hooker? True it was wartime, and the oldest profession was thriving. But child prostitution in a nice neighborhood? I found my arm waving and my mouth whistling the lovely vision to a halt. A rather rude method, I must admit.

BRUNO BERNARD

Above: Tempest Storm, striptease artist, 1952.

Opposite: Lili St. Cyr, exotic dancer, on stage at Ciro's nightclub, Hollywood, 1949.

Bernard
of
Hollywood

after sessions ... when she started to confide in me, especially after she heard that I too was brought up in an orphanage.)

She became my 'little sis' and I promised to help her all I could, which I did. She told me ."

BRUNO BERNARD

"I never really lived with my mother. I had . . . let's say, 10 or 11 foster families. She was put in a crazy house in Norwalk. You ever been to Norwalk, Mr. Bernard? I was told she had para . . . paranoid schizo . . . schizophrenia. My grandmother and grandfather died in one of those crazy places. I don't know when she went away, but I have dreams of her pushing me in a baby carriage and I'm wearing a pretty white dress."

"And your father, Norma Jean?"

"On the weekends, sometimes the foster families would sit me in a movie theater from morning till night." In the corner of her eye a tear appeared, "I'd watch Clark Gable and pretend he was my father . . ."

"Norma Jean told me there was a portrait of a smiling Gable tacked to her wall. Her secret father to take the illegitimacy away."

"'My mother's not dead!' I remember screaming," Norma said. 'I have a mother! Then after a while in the orphanage, I'd pretend she was dead. I cleaned toilets and worked in the kitchen washing dishes. There were a hundred of us. We made five cents a month. At night, when everyone was sleeping, I'd sit up in the window and cry. I'd look over in the distance and there was this tall water tower and on the top of it, it said 'RKO.' My mother had worked as a cutter at RKO. I can't see her face. She was a woman with red hair."

Above: Bruno Bernard's note on the day Norma Jean first came to his studio.

Opposite: Norma Jean, 1946.

Without warning, a social worker sent my brother Heinze, my sister Gerta, and me to three different orphanages because of the pitiful way we lived. This is a great shame in a Jewish family.

"You had a family, Mr. Bernard," Norma Jean wistfully sighs.

"The world is your oyster, Norma Jean. I was alone and penniless when I kissed the ground on Ellis Island. We are survivors, you and I."

This real-life Cinderella story transported me back to the newspaper and scrap metal route of my childhood in Berlin. It released my empathy for this girl born on the wrong side of the tracks who seemed hell-bent on making the American Dream come true for herself.

BRUNO BERNARD

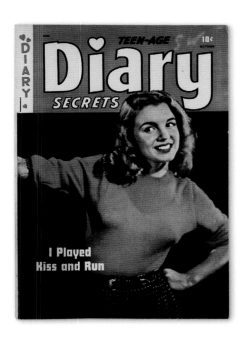

Opposite: Norma Jean, 1946.

Above: *Teen-Age Diary Secrets* magazine, photograph of Norma Jean, circa 1947. Photograph by Bruno Bernard.

Above and opposite: Norma Jean, 1946.

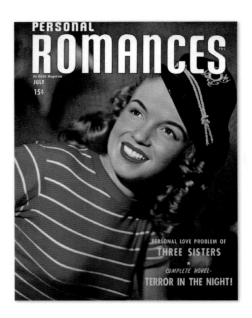

Above and opposite: Norma Jean, *Personal Romances* magazine, 1947 and outtakes from cover photoshoot.

From the initial sitting, I was able to place an advertisement with a pharmaceutical manufacturer depicting Norma Jean bandaging Rolf's "injured paw." The dog definitely stole the show, a fact that did not escape Norma Jean's critical judgment when she looked at the proof sheets. After she became Marilyn Monroe, she saw to it that nobody stole a scene from her again.

BRUNO BERNARD

Norma Jean, Griffith Park, Hollywood, California, 1946.

Before I finished putting my unwieldy 5-x-7 Eastman camera on its tripod, Norma Jean emerged from her large beach towel, ready for action.

I started giving her directions: "Would you please climb up on the front girder so I can get a better angle on your legs?"

"Oh, you want to make a Vargas girl out of me," Norma Jean commented knowingly. "All legs and a shrunken head. I know what you're up, to Mr. Bernard!"

"What's wrong with the Vargas girls?" I wanted to know.

"Not a thing. I wish I could look like his Ziegfeld beauties in *Esquire*—they're divine—but no real girl could ever look like those drawings, could she?"

"Not quite, but photographers can create a similar illusion by elongating the legs from a low perspective, but not so low as to distort the proportions of the head too much."

Her enthusiasm and tenacity are infectious. After hours of continuous shooting, she was still fresh.

BRUNO BERNARD

Above: Norma Jean, Griffith Park, Hollywood, California, 1946.
Opposite: Reverse side of photo with Bruno Bernard's notes and photo agency stamps;
Norma Jean, Griffith Park, Hollywood, California, 1946.

MARILYN MONROE,
Early Pin-Ups,

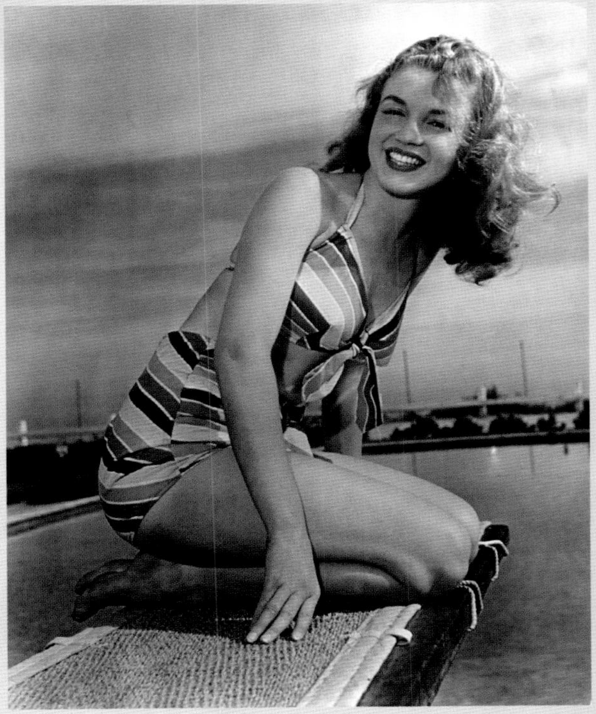

1946

Marilyn's good figure made her a good pin-up model, of which this photo is an early example. I Knever knew a more enthusiastic and cooperative model than Marilyn. Even at the end of the longest shooting session she would come up with fresh ideas. She also was prompt then and did not mind getting up at 5.30 in the morning so we could reach the Mount Wilson location by 7 o' clock.

2

2

M. Monroe

"I want to become a movie star!" she declared, swirling her hips. "It's been my dream since I was a kid. You've got to help me, Bernie," and she quickly took out my publicity brochure and repeated every word. "'Professional photography has as its prime purpose selling an actor or a professional performer to producers, directors and, of course, the public.' You've got to take a few more sexy photos of me," she insisted, making boring obscene gestures. "That will be my 'open sesame' to the studios."

"Norma, darling, whatever you do, never put hot on hot—that looks vulgar and would turn a real man off. Let your curves tell it all, and counteract the body language with a complete look of innocence. Your eyes should be asking, 'Why do men look at me?' Blend waif with Venus and you'll create combustion in photos."

BRUNO BERNARD

Above: Bernard of Hollywood's "Open Sesame" brochure, 1942.

Opposite: Norma Jean classic pin-up transparency with photo agency marks, 1946.

MARILYN MONROE
FIRST SITTING BY
BRUNO BERNARD

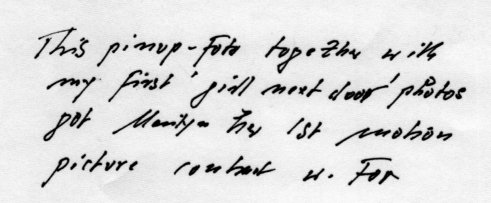

This pinup-foto together with my first 'girl next door' photos got Marilyn the 1st motion picture contract w. For

Opposite: Norma Jean classic pin-up photo, 1946.

Above: Reverse side of photograph, 1946; Robert Mitchum viewing the 1946
photograph of Marilyn (opposite page) in Bruno Bernard's 1950 portfolio
magazine *Pin-Ups: A Step Beyond.*

Above: Original negative sleeve with Bruno Bernard's notes which reads
"Similar pose was the cover of *LAFF*, which got Howard Hughes interested in MM," 1946.

Opposite: Norma Jean, photo used for the cover of *LAFF* magazine, 1946.

To me, she was the girl next door type. She had a peaches-and-cream complexion and that is when I took the pin-ups of her in a two-piece bathing suit, which believe it or not was daring at the time.

BRUNO BERNARD, 1984 INTERVIEW WITH MARIA SHRIVER
FOR "CBS MORNING NEWS," INTRODUCED BY DIANE SAWYER

Opposite: Norma Jean classic pin-up photo, 1946.

Above left: Postcard depicting Norma Jean, 1947.

Above right: Bruno Bernard's illustrated photography instruction guide, 1948.

My friend at 20th Century Fox, Ben, was so impressed with the color photos I sent him that he met with her today and wants to give her screen test option. He was struck by her beauty and childlike quality, the inexpensive cotton print dress encasing her "astonishing figure." Ben and I discussed our mutual concern for her high-pitched voice, and it was decided she should make a silent screen test. I, then, suggested how important it was, if possible, to shoot the test in color, since Zanuck had okayed it based on my color photographs. She needed as much going for her visually as possible, since we were both afraid of the fact that she didn't have any acting training - not even in high school.

Prosit! What timing! The *LA Times* today published a photo showing the RKO motion picture magnate Howard Hughes in an iron lung clutching the just-released *LAFF* magazine color pinup cover shot on Norma. In an accompanying story the notorious gossip columnist Hedda Hopper wrote, "Howard Hughes must be on the road to recovery. He turned over in his iron lung and wants to know more about the lovely cover girl, Norma Jean." I SOS'ed Darryl Zanuck and said, "I suggest you sign up the beautiful child-woman, Norma Jean Baker, before Howard Hughes does."

"What a gorgeous girl!" Zanuck declared. "Bernard, we're signing her to a studio stock contract."

BRUNO BERNARD

"Someday I'm going to have oodles and oodles of fan mail, just like Betty Grable."

MARILYN MONROE

Norma Jean in studio at Don Lee Television, 1946.

"Handling Marilyn's publicity is about as easy as guarding a bag of fleas. At photo sessions, I can never let her out of my sight for fear of her strip tease inclinations. The minute she spies a press photographer on our lot, she lifts her skirt and falls into a cheese cake pose . . . As you probably know, this gal always walks around without panties."

ROY CRAFT, MARILYN'S PERSONAL PUBLICIST AT FOX

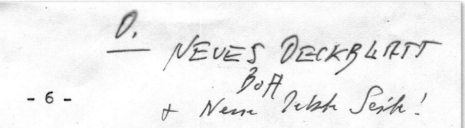

- 6 -

lap giving full view of her crossed legs. At the end of the three hours' session we still made a number of romance cover photos complete with basket cap and flowers in her hands to conform to the wanted stereotype of this period.

Left: Bruno Bernard's note.
Opposite: Norma Jean, 1946.

Two automatic photographic machines recently invented abroad were installed in Prague, which reproduced six or ten more exposures of the same person on a single print.

When I took such a series of photographs to Kafka I said light-heartedly: "For a couple of krone one can have oneself photographed from every angle. The apparatus is a mechanical Know-Thyself."

"You mean to say, Mistake-Thyself," said Kafka, with a faint smile.

I protested: "What do you mean? The camera cannot lie!"

"Who told you that?" Kafka leaned his head toward his shoulder. "Photography concentrates one's eye on the superficial. For that reason it obscures the hidden life which glimmers through the outlines of things like a play of light and shade. One can't catch that even with the sharpest lens. One has to grope for it by feeling…This automatic camera doesn't multiply men's eyes but only gives a fantastically simplified fly eye's view."

—Gustav Janouch, *Conversations with Kafka*, Prague 1921

"There's no such thing as chance.
It's all preordained. Like Kismet."

MARILYN MONROE

Norma Jean discovery series, first professional studio sitting, 1946.

CHAPTER 3

MARILYN AND JOHNNY 1949–1950

> The Palm Springs Racquet Club's tennis courts were swept clean when the voluptuous Marilyn posed in her body-hugging swimsuit and four-inch cork heels on the diving board.

BRUNO BERNARD

The mornings came with tears on pillows, fears and collective betrayals. Being dropped by Fox and the six-month Columbia Studio buildup coming to a halt was the least of it. Marilyn held her breath, waited for a revelation, wished on a star, pounded the streets, and exhausted her modeling agency. She showed up at Dad's studio, looking for a break, an assignment, some indication. Chance and timing had been their destiny. He had been commissioned to do a cover layout story at his home away from home, the Palms Springs Racquet Club, a destination for disappearance.

Left: Palm Springs Racquet Club entrance, 1948.

Opposite: Marilyn Monroe, Palm Springs Racquet Club, 1949.

In a mystical, sleepy little valley in 1934, actors Ralph Bellamy and Charles Farrell founded a hideaway for Hollywood. The stars were close enough to Hollywood and yet far away enough to have fun, let their hair down, roll up their shirtsleeves and simply be themselves, as opposed to their carefully orchestrated screen images.

The social climate of Hollywood's Golden Era reflected a postwar American optimism. These heroes were glamorized on the silver screen. It was a time and place when glamour was truly glamorous, and the stars behaved as such. The reigning studio system, which created these stars, was a prosperous business and dictated a strict lifestyle, an image, and ultimately an illusion.

Maria Shriver interviewing my dad for the CBS morning news asked,

> Would you like to create photographs of the stars now?

And dad replied,

> I would if they had the right attitude. They were very cooperative with me. The behavior was different because the whole climate, which was created by Hollywood, was different. Which was a great climate of artificiality, I must admit.

At the club the illustrious would consort with their peers, nurture discretely those private relationships on which their careers depended, and commence and end relationships that were symbols of romance in our minds. They felt safe and guarded from the flash bulbs and glare of the media spotlight. Dad was the only one given photographic privileges, since he was on a first-name basis with all and had established one of his three studios in the Springs. Charley would always say, "Don't worry, he's one of us. He will never release any photos that should not be published, but simply turn them over to the club for our family album."

The club was sprinkled with tight-eyed, tanned, saddle-skinned, Eastern money, white and diamond-wearing stars. Katherine Hepburn and Spencer Tracy. Clark Gable taking a shot of a Pimm's cup at the Bamboo Bar. Gene Tierney lounging on aqua and meeting Oleg Cassini. Joan Crawford looking upset after spotting Ginger Rogers looking happy with Joan's ex beau. Rita Hayworth in the locker room.

It was in the Springs one auspicious morning, that Marilyn, smelling like baby powder, was unloaded along with the camera equipment from Dad's station wagon. This magical photo safari would change the course of her life forever, when Dad introduced her to Johnny Hyde, vice president of the William Morris Agency, who fell head over heels for her.

Above: Original negative and sleeve, 1949.
Opposite: Marilyn Monroe, Palm Springs Racquet Club, 1949.

The pinups I took of Marilyn at the Racquet

50%

Club in Palm Springs — when I introduced her to the mighty motion picture agent Johnny Hyde, who sparkplugged her career.

"Who's this gorgeous dame . . . your girlfriend?" I knew at that instant this could only have been Johnny Hyde, a vice president at William Morris, a shrimp in stature, but long in connections. I felt annoyed at what he was implying. He asked if I would mind taking a few snapshots for private use.

In Marilyn's present state of unemployment, this introduction to Johnny was welcome . . . The dream world she had erected with such inventiveness and persistence had collapsed. The Fox production found her NT (No Talent), a handicap, too much of a risk for a "big buildup" and did not exercise her studio contract option.

BRUNO BERNARD

Above: Marilyn Monroe, Palm Springs Racquet Club, 1949.

Opposite: Transparency.

"Trust you don't mind me taking a few snaps strictly for private use!" Without waiting for an answer to his rhetorical question, Johnny made a quick dash to his bungalow adjacent to the pool and stormed out armed with a Leica and several telephoto lenses. To the amusement of all bystanders, the former circus acrobat-turned-agent crouched on his belly and fired away from his frog perspective as if Eastman Kodak would go out of business tomorrow. After he had shot his bolt of 36 exposures he ran back to his bungalow for more ammunition.

This interlude prompted Marilyn to ask, "Who is this jerk snapping all of these pictures?"

"This jerk is Johnny Hyde, an ardent amateur photographer. Professionally, he happens to be vice president of the William Morris Agency," I whispered in her ear. After this input, I might just as well have packed my camera gear.

BRUNO BERNARD

Marilyn Monroe, Palm Springs, 1949.

Johnny would not permit me to take any more pictures of Marilyn in a two-piece bathing suit, which, ironically, had endeared her to him only a few months before.

BRUNO BERNARD

PICTORIAL
COPYRIGHT PHOTO
REPRODUCTION FEE PAYABLE TO
PICTORIAL PRESS LIMITED
13 BERNERS STREET, LONDON W1P 3DE
T: 01-255-1468 TX: 264876 FAX:01-836-0974
VAT NO 243 4730 79

1947

COPYRIGHT:
BERNARD OF HOLLYWOOD
5504 Evergreen Ave.
Las Vegas — Nevada

ORIGINAL PRINT
NOT FOR YOUR FILES
RETURN IMMEDIATELY
AFTER PUBLICATION.

/3

ORIGINAL PRINT
MUST BE RETURNED

13 Johnny was Marilyn's Professor Higgins, he revamped her completely from the loveable, carefree all American girl to the
breathtakingly beautiful but dumb Hollywood Blonde, a type
which could be sold much easier to the studios and the masses.

Page 2 Captions.

13 ctd An ironic touch was that Johnny did not permit me to
photograph Marilyn in a bikini any longer, reasoning
solemnly 'her pin-up days are over', 'she will be an
actress from now on!'

Above: Reverse side of photograph with Bruno Bernard's notes and photo agency stamps, 1947.

Opposite: Marilyn Monroe, Palm Springs Racquet Club, 1949.

Following pages: Marilyn and Johnny Hyde, vice president of the William Morris Agency, poolside and on New Year's Eve, 1949.

Her goal was to be a movie star. It was not money.

She turned down money from Johnny.

BRUNO BERNARD

Johnny Hyde dances with Marilyn Monroe
auf der New Year's Eve Party in the
Racquet Club of Palm Springs

XXXX

NORMAN R. BROKAW
CHAIRMAN OF THE BOARD

December 13, 2007

Dear Susan and Josh,

Once again, you have made this holiday season a big winner. I love the pictures each year of Marilyn and this year is no exception.

It seems like yesterday that I remember so often being with her and taking her to different places for auditions such as 20th Century Fox and also, on occasion, dropping her off to be photographed by your father. Whenever I look at some of these photos which I have in my home, I cherish every one of them but I also cherish the extreme thoughtfulness of you and Josh for giving me the opportunity to relive this wonderful part of my life. I have just finished my 65th year here at WMA and, because of memories like these, I am planning not to retire at this time.

As I've told you before, I remember introducing Marilyn to Joe DiMaggio at the Brown Derby in Hollywood. What really happened is I took her down to KNBH which was located at Vine Street. She did a scene for "Lights, Camera, Action" and whoever did the best scene won the prize of the evening. It was Marilyn. So afterwards, to celebrate, I took her to the Brown Derby and while sitting there, Bill Frawley, one of our clients, said that he was sitting with the great Joe DiMaggio who would love to meet the young lady but you know he's shy. Could you stop by on the way out? That's when I took Marilyn by his table and they met. I'm sure you remember that Marilyn lived for quite some time in my uncle Johnny Hyde's house and my grandmother lived there too so we got to be Marilyn's extended family.

Thank you both so much for your wonderful gift and I send my warmest wishes for a happy holiday season

Fondly,

NRB/mf

Ms. Susan Bernard
Mr. Josh Miller

Johnny obtained for Marilyn, her first really good part, "Angela," a gangster's moll in the MGM film, *The Asphalt Jungle*. So anxious to obtain the part, was this girl with the most perfect figure, and so insecure, she put falsies in her bra for the film test. She studied each of her lines diligently with her coach Natasha Lytess, who had taken Marilyn under her wing after her short stay at Columbia.

BRUNO BERNARD

Asphalt Jungle. It called for an angel faced blonde with a wickedly curvaceous figure

She came to the test made up as a tart, with falsies. — He had to strip down all the way down to get the basic girl, the real quality, the true Lolita quality

Opposite: Thank you letter to Susan Bernard and son, Joshua, from Norman Brokaw, CEO of the William Morris Agency and nephew of Johnny Hyde, 2007.

Above: Marilyn and director John Huston on the set of *The Asphalt Jungle*, 1950.

David Wills Collection.

A cosmetic surgeon in the Springs had restyled her nose and straightened the facial tissues under her skin. Under his tutelage, the changeover from the natural nice girl next door to the siren, Marilyn, was complete.

BRUNO BERNARD

Johnny arranged the nose job.

Above: Bruno Bernard's book, *Beauty Was Their Destiny*, 1981.
Opposite: Marilyn Monroe, 1950.

Marilyn called me crying out of control.

"He's got all these tubes running through him, Bernie, and they've got him under a big oxygen tent," Marilyn blurted out to me through the phone.

"Who, Marilyn, who?" I asked.

"Johnny! He had a heart attack in Palm Springs."

"Marilyn, listen to me carefully," I said slowly. "You are not in a state to drive."

"If anything happens to Johnny," Marilyn whispered, her voice beginning to crack, "I can't go on without him."

The indefatigable Johnny, obtained a copy of the uncut scenes from *The Asphalt Jungle*, made a rough cut himself, and projected it for his pal Joe Schenck in his penthouse. Within days of having a massive heart attack, Johnny negotiated a seven-year contract with Fox for Marilyn.

BRUNO BERNARD

Opposite: Marilyn Monroe, 1950.

Right: Postcard, 1950.

CHAPTER 4

FAME
1951–1953

Marilyn learned to wear mink and white fox. Make her eyes the color of dumb blonde, a sad baby blue. Be liquid and pour herself into gowns. Sip champagne and walk. She learned to realize the extent of her fame and laugh. Spring into cars and limos, hide in doorways, not talk to strangers. Strangers were unpredictable, they asked for an autograph, a favor, a photo, wrote letters proposing marriage and sent pubic hair.

She unabashedly threw herself into the sensuality of her body, took pleasure in men desiring her, it amused, and excited her. If men in trucks whistled at her, shouting, "Hey, Marilyn, we love you!" it was fine. Just like, when she was Norma Jean, the teenager, smiling and giggling, when Dad whistled to catch her attention. She was well aware of her power over others. She needed the proof of being loved; it temporarily erased her fears of once being unwanted. Being loved by her public saved her.

Identity Crisis between Norma Jean + Marilyn.

Above: Bruno Bernard's note.

Opposite: Marilyn Monroe, Niagara Falls, 1952.

Marilyn's nude calendar appeared without warning on garage walls and under men's pillows.

Life magazine reproduced the incriminating nude. Overnight, the Marilyn nude appeared on every household item, from service trays, to lampshades, matchboxes, playing cards, and notebooks. Marilyn was held silent.

The puritanical Hays commission ruled like Nazis banging on doors. Artistic freedom was stifled and censored. Fox Studios' multi-million-dollar investment in Marilyn's unreleased films was in jeopardy. Darryl Zanuck stopped production on *Don't Bother to Knock,* her first serious dramatic part.

During this period, Dad was defending and winning court cases against the religious right in Boston. He had pioneered the novel approach to the art of pin-up photography along with Vargas and others, daring to prove "a woman in scant attire need not be perceived as vulgar display of the feminine body, but rather as a legitimate work of art transmitting aesthetic values," just as Hearst distributed, to artistic acclaim, the pre-Playboy *Bernard of Hollywood's Pin-Ups: A Step Beyond.*

The studio held a carefully orchestrated press conference. Marilyn stood up in front of the reporters enjoying her femininity. This was way before the equality and emancipation promised by Women's Liberation. Marilyn simply told them she had to eat and pay the rent, and it was honest work, and the human body is nothing to be ashamed of. Ironically, this sentiment became the battle cry of the movement a decade later. In the split second of a shutter's speed, flashbulbs popped, sounding like broken glass and recorded her mortality, vulnerability, and mutability.

Left: Marilyn Monroe pin-up, 1952

Above: Marilyn and co-star Richard Widmark, *Don't Bother to Knock,* 195

Overnight Marilyn had become everyone's orphaned little sis; the protective instinct in millions of big brothers had been aroused. Marilyn sat in the goddesses' pantheon. Myths thrive on controversy. She had also created an obstacle course for Fox. How were they to transform the sexuality of her infamous nude calendar into flesh and blood person on screen? Across the Atlantic, under perfumed skies, and in smoky dark cinemas, Brigitte Bardot's child-woman persona was permitted without censorship. Romance and lust were inseparable.

Marilyn could have recited the telephone directory backwards and received a legion of worshippers. *How to Marry a Millionaire* and *Gentlemen Prefer Blondes* brought in hundreds of millions of dollars. And the conflict of a fabricated myth left Marilyn in a constant state of anxiety and confusion over the identity she had created.

Right: Marilyn Monroe pin-up, 1952.

For our sitting, she brought an edition of Rilke's poems, which I had given her last year. I was amazed how she started to read in German—in her Gentlemen Prefer Blondes Lorelei voice, as she called it—a poem "Madness." The girl in the poem is as mad as Ophelia. Marilyn's selection of this morbid subject seemed strange to me at the time when a bright future seemed to be within her grasp.

"One night I might read my poems to you if you promise not to laugh at me."

"Promise!"

I knew then that Norma Jean was not dead, she was only in hiding under net stockings.

"The Madness"

She's always pondering: I am... I am...
Who do you think you are, *Marie*?
A Queen, a Queen!
On your knee (in front of me) On your knee

She always need to cry, I was... I was...
Who were you then Marie?
A no one's child, very poor and alone,
And I can't tell you how.

And you became out of that Child a
Princess, to whom one kneels?
Because everything is different now,
Than what a beggar see's.

Thats how the Things have brought you to such heights,
And can you still say when?
One night, One night, over another night,-
And they spoke to me differently.
I stepped out into the alley/street and saw,
That it was strung with strings,
Marie became melody, melody...
And danced from edge to edge.
The people crept fearfully towards it,
As if they had been attached to the house,
Than only a Queen is allowed,
To dance in the streets/alley: Dance...

Her childhood dreams were realized. But what happened to Norma Jean? The fierce battle between two antagonists in her soul was about to unfold.

BRUNO BERNARD

Marilyn Monroe, 1953.

On the other side, they had to play down Marilyn's sexuality because of the pressure of the church and women's clubs. To make their superstar palatable to these groups, they brought Norma Jean to the surface, the harmless and helpless orphan who was adopted as America's 'li'l sis'. In this fashion, Fox succeeded years ahead of 'Foggy Bottom' in producing a 'clean bomb'; something that became an integral part of the Monroe mystique.

Marilyn herself enjoyed the masquerade greatly. Even as a child she had given her foster mother, Grace McKee, a gala performance after each visit to the neighborhood movie house, playing the different roles of the entire cast. Today, in the age of the electronic babysitter, almost any toddler can duplicate the same feat.

Marilyn herself frequently mixed up her on and off screen characters. In the former television quiz game, To Tell The Truth, one of the three male or female contestants was the real Mr. or Mrs. X. The other two were, of course, lying and the panel had to find out who was the genuine article. Marilyn played this type of game to the hilt in her life. In fact, she considerably enlarged the number of her self-roles until she had a large repertoire to correspond to her various moods. In one of her frank conversations with the London journalist, Frank Weatherby, she freely discussed the 'pattern of her selves' and wondered how people could make the mistake of thinking of themselves as one consistent self during their entire lives.

Above: Bruno Bernard's notes.
Opposite left: Marilyn Monroe calendar, photograph by Tom Kelly, originally printed in 1950.
Opposite top: excerpt from *Tell it to Louella*, 1961.
Opposite bottom: *Variety* headline, circa 1950.

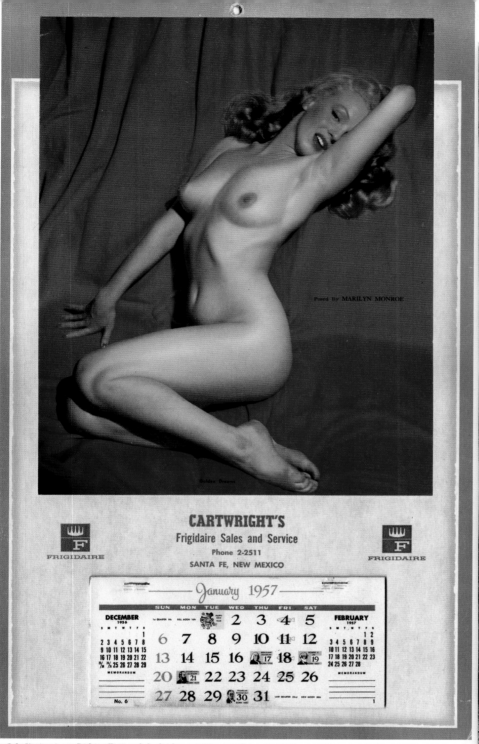

Posed by MARILYN MONROE

Golden Dreams

CARTWRIGHT'S
Frigidaire Sales and Service
Phone 2-2511

FRIGIDAIRE · FRIGIDAIRE

SANTA FE, NEW MEXICO

January 1957

DECEMBER 1956	SUN	MON	TUE	WED	THU	FRI	SAT	FEBRUARY 1957
S M T W T F S			1	2	3	4	5	S M T W T F S
1	6	7	8	9	10	11	12	1 2
2 3 4 5 6 7 8	13	14	15	16	17	18	19	3 4 5 6 7 8 9
9 10 11 12 13 14 15	20	21	22	23	24	25	26	10 11 12 13 14 15 16
16 17 18 19 20 21 22	27	28	29	30	31			17 18 19 20 21 22 23
23/30 24/31 25 26 27 28 29								24 25 26 27 28
MEMORANDUM								MEMORANDUM

No. 6

'Marilyn's Hidden Torment'

She Triumphs Over 'Calendar Scandal'

The Marilyn Monroe whose sexy smile flashes from the screen is a very different woman than the actress who goes before the camera — just how different is told in this fourth article of a series on the star and her troubles.

By LOUELLA O. PARSONS

Copyright, 1961, by Louella O. Parsons. From the book "Tell It to Louella." Published by G. P. Putnam's Sons. Distributed by King Features Syndicate.

My daughter Harriet was producing "Clash by Night" at RKO, starring Barbara Stanwyck, Paul Douglas and Robert Ryan, and there was a smaller —but very important—role still to be cast.

Harriet arranged to borrow Marilyn from Fox. She heard me talk about Marilyn, but she wasn't quite prepared for her.

While this picture was being made, she began that habit of tardiness which has since become constant. It was only a matter of minutes at this time; nothing like what developed later.

(I have heard that she reported on the lot while "Some Like It Hot" was being made at 6 p.m. to answer a 10 a.m. call.)

And she insisted upon her own dramatic coach, Natasha Lytess, to give her direction. There were times too when she asked for retakes though everyone else was satisfied with a scene.

DEEP CHANGES

It was, as Harriet told me, more annoying than anything else. But it was a sign that

couldn't bring herself to her place before the camera.

She would be late getting to the studio. Then she would delay, for every conceivable and some inconceivable reason, the moment when she went before the camera.

This was the period when she started seeing baseball star Joe DiMaggio. And here was a contradiction.

She had always had a penchant for older men whose interests were, at least in part, intellectual. Joe was certainly older and while he was a nice guy and an all-round sports hero, he hardly qualified as an egghead.

The thought came to me that perhaps Marilyn, now established as star, might have decided to leave the books to the libraries.

NEW COURTSHIP

MARILYN MONROE, GIRL PRESIDENT, TELLS OF HER CONTRACT DEMAND

By FRED HIFT

Clad in white satin and wrapped in ermine, a demure Marilyn Monroe in N. Y. last week (7) had a surprise script ready for 20th-Fox. Plot involved her "Declaration of Independence" from the studio and from the type of roles she's been playing to date.

Delaney's Views

Crux of the contract issue involving Marilyn Monroe appears to be the manner, if any, in which the original contract was terminated. It runs to 1958, with yearly options. As Delaney explained it Monday

No Serial Number on Stub; New Ticket Thwarts Any 'Checkers' of Attendance

Minneapolis, Jan. 11.
North Central Allied in its cur

"The truth about Marilyn Monroe is that she was *saved* by Hollywood. Fame saved her. The spotlight beating on her 24 hours a day made the world seem livable to her. She lived in the midst of her fame as though she were more a poster than a woman, but the unreality never hurt her. It was the only world in which she could thrive. The real world held only hobgoblins for her, terrors that harried her nights. The movies did not destroy Marilyn; they gave her a long and joyous reprieve from the devils which hounded her in earlier years, and which came back to hound her in the end . . ."

BEN HECHT, SCREENWRITER

Here and previoius pages: publicity photoshoot, circa 1951.

Bernard
of
Hollywood

Opposite: publicity photo, circa 1951.

Above: publicity pin-up photos, circa 1951.

Marilyn was in seventh heaven again—seeing her name up in lights on a motion picture marquee was the best medicine for her after the long months mourning Johnny. Through her photographs she was becoming the best-known unknown player long before becoming a star. She is in such high spirits that she climbed high on the top of a ladder and pointed proudly to her name on the marquee advertising *As Young As You Feel*.

"Look at Marilyn up there," she mused, referring to her motion picture character in the third person. "She's bigger than me. I wish it said Norma Jean, then everybody at the orphanage would know it's me. Soon people will turn their heads when I walk down Hollywood Boulevard and they'll say to each other, 'Yes, that's her, that's Marilyn.'"

BRUNO BERNARD

176: Her lack of education and her sem-blance of naivety had persuaded most of the fox executives that she did not have the intelligence to guide her own career.

Above: Bruno Bernard's note.

Opposite: Marilyn with poster for *As Young as You Feel*, 1951.

In Hollywood, there is the story and then there are the facts—at least that's what famous band leader Ray Anthony implied when I interviewed him over the phone and asked, "Could you tell me about the party when Marilyn wore her pink dress from *Niagara* and Mickey Rooney was there?"

"Susan, do you want the story, or do you want the facts?"

"I want what really happened, Ray."

"I threw a party at my house for Marilyn. It was a big publicity party Fox and my publicist, Red Doff, threw in 1952. I wrote a song, "Marilyn." She was very gracious and took pictures with everyone. There was this helicopter and *Look* magazine was going to cover it from the sky. There was a down draft and the helicopter started falling. Luckily, there was a big open space at my home and the helicopter could safely land. There were international photographers, 500 people at the party, and the press started shooting pictures of Marilyn and me, and the Navy helicopter guy. There was traffic held up on Ventura Boulevard for hours."

"What about Mickey Rooney?" I asked.

"Oh, Mickey showed up at every party."

"I heard Marilyn arrived in the helicopter."

"Not true."

Above: Marilyn at party thrown by bandleader Ray Anthony at his California home, 1953.

Opposite: From left: Helicopter pilot, Marilyn and Ray Anthony, 1953.

Above: original contact shee

Opposite: color transparenc

Marilyn inherited Betty Grable's dressing room on the lot, a dream she had coveted since her days as an unknown. But she hadn't inherited Betty's equanimity begotten by the creative satisfaction of her film work, and her happy family life.

BRUNO BERNARD

Opposite: From left: Mickey Rooney, Marilyn, and Ray Anthony, 1953.

Above: Marilyn at party thrown by bandleader Ray Anthony at his California home, 1953.

Natasha Lytess, acting coach and mentor: "Bernie, you as a Reinhardt student, will understand what I mean, when I tell you that the studio big shots and the American public does not know the real Marilyn yet. All they see is her super structure, the smaller part of a sailboat vessel above the water, while the larger and weightier part is below the surface. I have been reading with Marilyn some of the best dramas of world literature and some outstanding novels . . . a film version of *The Brothers Karamazov* is now being prepared. Marilyn would be an ideal Gershenka. You've known Marilyn from the beginning, do you agree?

Marilyn Monroe: "I'll make the studio fat heads cry one day, if they don't let me play Gershenka."

Spyrous Skouras, President of 20th Century Fox: "Baby forget the sentimentalities. You make money only with your tits and your ass. . . . Your talent is located above your waist and below your navel."

Deep down in her psyche gnawed a dissatisfaction with her fame, based solely on her physical attributes, rather than her acting talent

Marilyn was devastated, and was more determined than ever to fight it out with the studio, but for the time being, she was enjoying a happy period in her private life, through her whirlwind romance with American sports idol, the baseball king, Joe Di Maggio.

BRUNO BERNARD

Above: *Piccolo* magazine, 1953.
Opposite: Marilyn, Niagara Falls, New York, 1952.

Bernard of Hollywood

"Whatever the reasons, her inability to have a child was to loom as a crucial disappointment in her life. The love goddess, the woman supreme, unable to create a baby; it was a dagger at her ego. There was something wrong with her; inside her, a defect, an evil. Nor would pills erase this sense of failure. Despite all, she yearned to be a mother, even if it meant temporarily putting films aside. She desperately wanted that fulfillment."

NORMAN ROSTEN

Marilyn at St. Jude Children's Hospital charity event, Hollywood Bowl, 1953.

"It takes me five hours to become Marilyn."

MARILYN MONROE

When she became Marilyn, contrary to all glib declarations by some of her associates that she was an invention, she invested that new creature with a sense of reality and purpose she had never felt in her previous life.

Above: Bruno Bernard's note.

Opposite: Marilyn at St. Jude Children's Hospital charity event, Hollywood Bowl, 1953.

"On the surface, she was still a happy girl. But those who criticized her never saw her as I did, crying like a baby because she often felt herself so inadequate. Sometimes she suffered terrific depressions, and would even talk about death. Occasionally, when she had one of these spells at home, she'd telephone me in the middle of the night, and I'd talk her out of it; or when I couldn't and was afraid she'd do what she finally did, I'd get dressed, drive to her place and talk to her. She had this great fear of becoming mentally unbalanced like her mother . . ."

WILLIAM TRAVILLA, COSTUME DESIGNER

Marilyn at St. Jude Children's Hospital charity event, Hollywood Bowl, 1953.

Her expression and moods were as vital as the rush of Niagara. Marilyn was never more vibrant than onstage and backstage at the Hollywood Bowl, in her Lorelei dress from *Gentlemen Prefer Blondes,* to raise funds devoted to the St. Jude Hospital for underprivileged children, a charity close to her heart.

BRUNO BERNARD

ORIGINAL PRINT MUST BE RETURNED

Pictorial Press Ltd.
3 SALISBURY COURT
FLEET STREET LONDON EC4

COPYRIGHT:
BERNARD OF HOLLYWOOD
5504 Evergreen Ave.
Las Vegas — Nevada

PICTORIAL
COPYRIGHT PHOTO
REPRODUCTION FEE PAYABLE TO
PICTORIAL PRESS LIMITED
13 BERNERS STREET, LONDON W1P 3DE
T: 01-255-1468 TX: 264876 FAX:01-836-0974
VAT NO 243 4730 79

ORIGINAL PRINT MUST BE RETURNED

These photos taken within seconds from each other backstage at the Hollywood Bowl where all showbusiness greats performed for a charity affair show clearly Marilyn's dual personality. In photo 17 Marilyn shows clearly stage fright as the veteran funny man Danny Kaye attempts to give her a few pointers.
In picture 18 Marilyn has spied the camera and beams her official smile while Danny genuinely enjoys the antics of his fellow comedian Danny Thomas onstage.

17/18

MARILYN MONROE,
Candids.

Reverse side of photograph with Bruno Bernard's notes and photo agency stamps, 1953.

Top left: Red Buttons, Marilyn and Danny Thomas at St. Jude Children's Hospital charity event, Hollywood Bowl, 1953.

Left: Marilyn and Danny Kaye, 1953.

Above: Original contact sheet, 1953.

"Mitch is one of the most interesting, fascinating men I have ever known."

MARILYN MONROE

Above: Marilyn at St. Jude Children's Hospital charity event, Hollywood Bowl, 1953.

Opposite: Marilyn and Robert Mitchum, 1953.

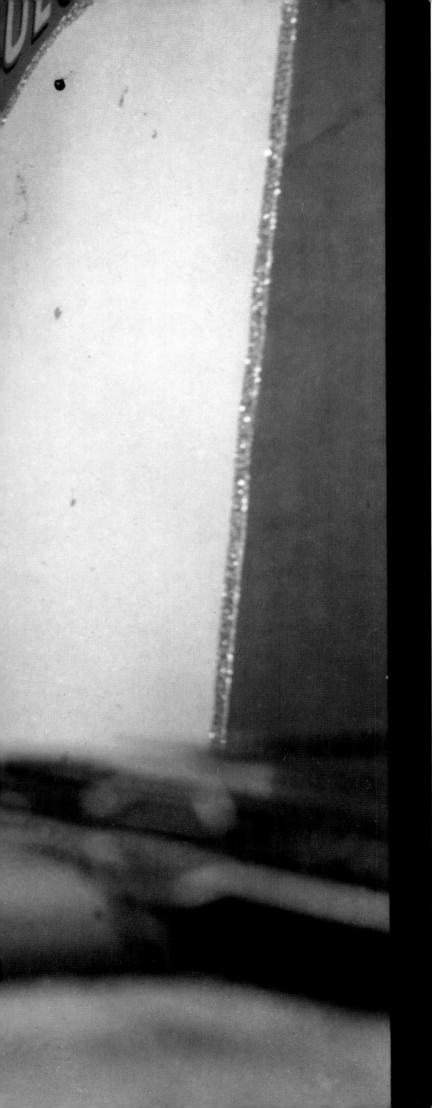

157-7

157-6

157-5

Opposite: Marilyn at St. Jude Children's Hospital charity event, Hollywood Bowl, 1953.

Above: Original contact sheet, 1953.

"... and I want to say that the people— if I am a star—the people made me a star—no studio, no person, but the people did."

MARILYN MONROE

Above and opposite: Marilyn at St. Jude Children's Hospital charity event, Hollywood Bowl

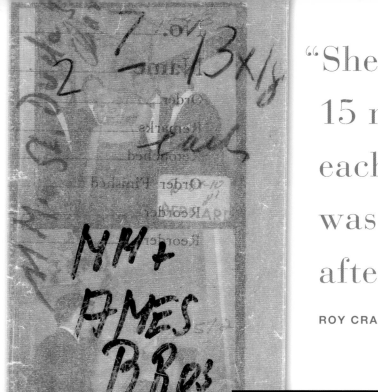

> "She had such magnetism that if 15 men were in a room with her, each man would be convinced he was the one she'd be waiting for after the others left."
>
> ROY CRAFT, MARILYN'S PRESS AGENT

Above left: Original negative sleeve, 1953.
Above right: Original contact sheet with Bruno Bernard's crop marks, 1953.
Opposite: Marilyn and Ames Brothers at St. Jude Children's Hospital charity event, Hollywood Bowl, 1953.

"I think she's something different to each man, blending somehow the things he seems to require most. . . . Marilyn is kind of ultimate, in her way, with a million sides to her. She is uniquely feminine. Everything she does is different, strange and exciting, from the way she talks to the way she uses that magnificent torso. She makes a man proud to be a man."

CLARK GABLE

Marilyn and Ronald Reagan, then president of the Screen Actors Guild, 1952.

"I feel that beauty and femininity are ageless and can't be contrived, and glamour—although manufacturers won't like this—cannot be manufactured. Not real glamour, it's based on femininity. I think that sexuality is only attractive when it's natural and spontaneous. This is where a lot of them miss the boat. And then something I just like to spout off on. We all are born sexual creatures, thank God, but it's a pity so many people despise and crush this natural gift. Art, real art, comes from it—everything."

MARILYN MONROE, 1962

Marilyn, *There's No Business Like Show Business*, 1954.

CHAPTER 5

THE BEGINNING OF THE END HOLLYWOOD, 1954

They were doomed from the beginning. You could say that fame was the cause. Her fame. His. They didn't have a chance. And yet, they were the great American love story—Marilyn and Joe. The romance played out like fiction. It was inevitable that fiction and fame would shadow the truth. They were the best thing that ever happened to one another.

M: Cinderella lives happily ever after only in the Fairy Tale. In real life — no matter how many clothes she puts on — or takes off — her heart remains embittered — and her spirit soiled by the ashes she swept in childhood.

Above: Bruno Bernard's note.
Opposite: Marilyn and attorney Jerry Geisler driving away after press conference in Hollywood announcing her divorce from Joe DiMaggio, 1954.

NEW YORK—

I really need this portrait sitting of Joe and Marilyn to tie in the cover with my layout. From the hall outside their suite at the St. Regis, I could hear a heated quarrel followed by her hysterical crying. I left, and never got my sitting. Without a suitable cover photo, my *Redbook* editor would ax the layout. I was downcast and silent. Roy ran into me in the elevator and attempted to console me. "All is not lost, Bernie, old pal, because the outside noise was so loud, Wilder has decided to reshoot the entire scene in Hollywood."

BACK IN HOLLYWOOD—

Marilyn's been heavily sedated. I haven't been able to reach her on the phone, or break through the cordon of her retinue. Days are passing without a response from her. In the meantime, the Trans-Lux Theatre and the adjoining Lexington Avenue stores are being rebuilt on the Fox lot. I'm beginning to get concerned, not only about a set appointment for my cover portrait, but about Marilyn's fragile emotional state now being manipulated by self-serving strangers. I'm sending to her home a set of her color Norma Jean first sitting as a memento. I'm writing a message, our familiar Maurois aphorism, "When you attain success, retain the qualities that brought you success."

BRUNO BERNARD

Opposite: 1946 photograph that Bruno Bernard sent Marilyn from one of their first sittings to remind her to "retain the qualities that brought you success."

Following pages: Hollywood press gathered at Marilyn's home for the announcement of her divorce from Joe DiMaggio, 1954.

Billy has ordered a closed set. "Out of regard for your long acquaintance with Marilyn, I'll permit you to come on the set tomorrow," publicist Harry Brand told me. I raced to the studio the next morning. The guard at the studio gate told me that the filming had been canceled.

I phoned Marilyn's house and the publicity department. No one answered. Feeling completely dejected, I drove home unconsciously taking the route via Palm Drive and saw the biggest assembly of Hollywood press I had ever seen in my Hollywood career. I quickly parked my car and raced with my camera to find the sad news that Marilyn would be coming out of her home any minute to announce her separation or divorce from Joe.

BRUNO BERNARD

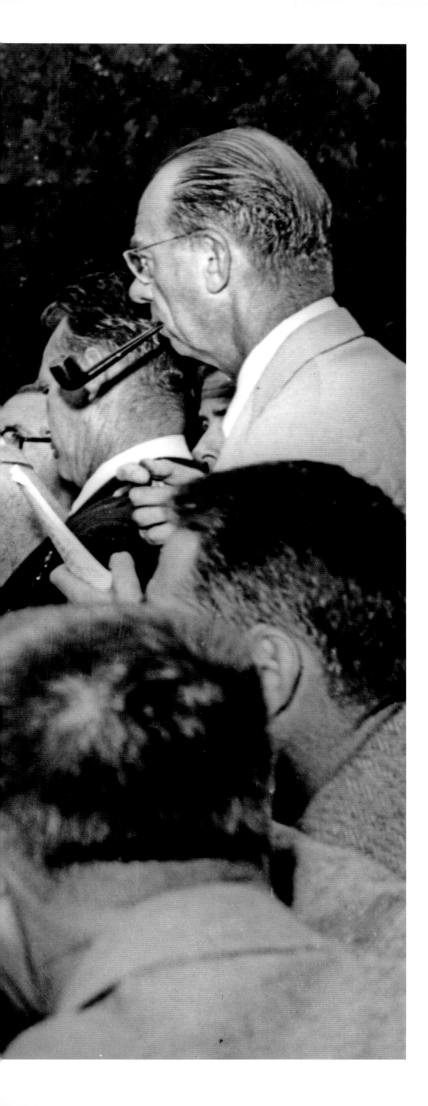

"I never loved
anyone more than Joe."

MARILYN MONROE

Marilyn and her attorney, Jerry Geisler, with Hollywood reporters, 1954.

> We understood each other momentarily as we had so often in the past. As Marilyn listlessly withdrew her hand to dry her tears—real ones, not glycerine—I shot the naked human creature behind the goddess. The fragile doll of Offenbach's *Tales of Hoffman*. It was the beginning of the end.

BRUNO BERNARD

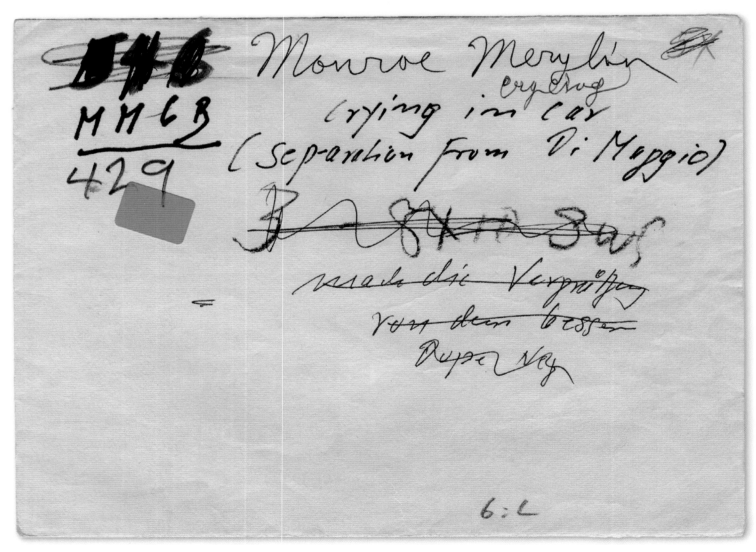

Above: Original photo sleeve, 1954.

Opposite: Marilyn on the day of her divorce announcement from Joe DiMaggio, 1954.

Her breakup with Joe had washed away not only the mascara, but also the mark of the plastic superstar, uncovering the fragile Norma Jean. A few days after her announcement to the press, Fox expected her on the Hollywood set to wrap up *The Seven Year Itch*.

When the green light blinked at the iron door of the huge Stage 3 on the Fox lot and I entered the set, I saw an exact replica of the Trans Lux Theatre and the storefronts. Billy Wilder was giving Marilyn suggestions for the thirty-fifth take of the skirt-blowing scene, while her stand-in was wearing long black toreador pants to prevent her from getting a cold.

BRUNO BERNARD

Above: Bruno Bernard's handwritten note.

Opposite: Marilyn and director Billy Wilder, Hollywood set, *The Seven Year Itch*, 1954.

"Any little thing I did for her, she was so appreciative. She treated me more like a friend than a studio associate. Before I would go into a scene to stand in for her, she would come over and fix my hair and clothes and she'd give me the motivation for the scene, so I would know what I was doing. She was my Paula Strasberg."

EVELYN MORIARTY, MARILYN'S STAND-IN

Stand-ins for Tom Ewell and Marilyn, Hollywood set, *The Seven Year Itch*, 1954.

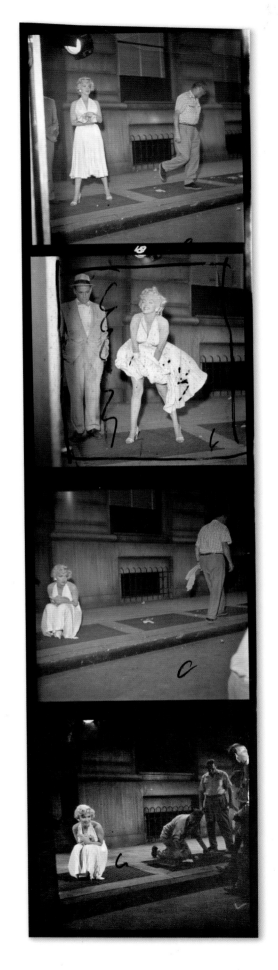

Above: Original contact sheet with Bruno Bernard's crop marks, 1954.

Opposite and following pages: Marilyn, Hollywood set, *The Seven Year Itch*, 1954.

Above and left: Marilyn and co-star Tom Ewell, Hollywood set, 1954.

Opposite: Marilyn, Hollywood set, *The Seven Year Itch*, 1954.

"I call the color of my hair
'Pillow Case White.'"

MARILYN MONROE

Marilyn and hairdresser Gladys Whitten, 1954.

When Marilyn's hairdresser Gladys Whitten combed her hair very carefully, Natasha acted as a second director, mesmerizing, articulating each syllable of her lines and emphasizing them through corresponding gestures. Marilyn concentrated on the hypnotic input, as if in a trance. When the camera rolled Natasha stood very close, just slightly out of camera range in order to lend moral support to her insecure puppet.

BRUNO BERNARD

Opposite: Marilyn with Natasha Lytess, 1954.

Above: Marilyn with mentor and acting coach Natasha Lytess and hairdresser Gladys Whitten, 1954.

Her drama coach Natasha Lytess is happy that the film is in the can

Above: Marilyn with Natasha Lytess, 1954.

Below: Natasha Lytess smiling at Marilyn from behind cameraman, 1954; Bruno Bernard's note.

Opposite: Marilyn with Natasha Lytess, 1954.

This strange entr'acte of the odd couple resembled more the rehearsal for a marionette show than the shooting of a film scene. In the final analysis it was the "absurd theater" within the make-believe world of movie land and was infinitely more interesting to watch than the edited film on screen. It gave me the key to understanding Marilyn's complete dependence on Natasha as if she were her mother and later on Paula Strasberg.

After the fortieth take, the director shouted enthusiastically, "Cut! Print it! This is it!"

Natasha came running towards Marilyn, embracing her jubilantly while the star, looking lost, asked her mom, "Do you really think I got it this time?"

BRUNO BERNARD

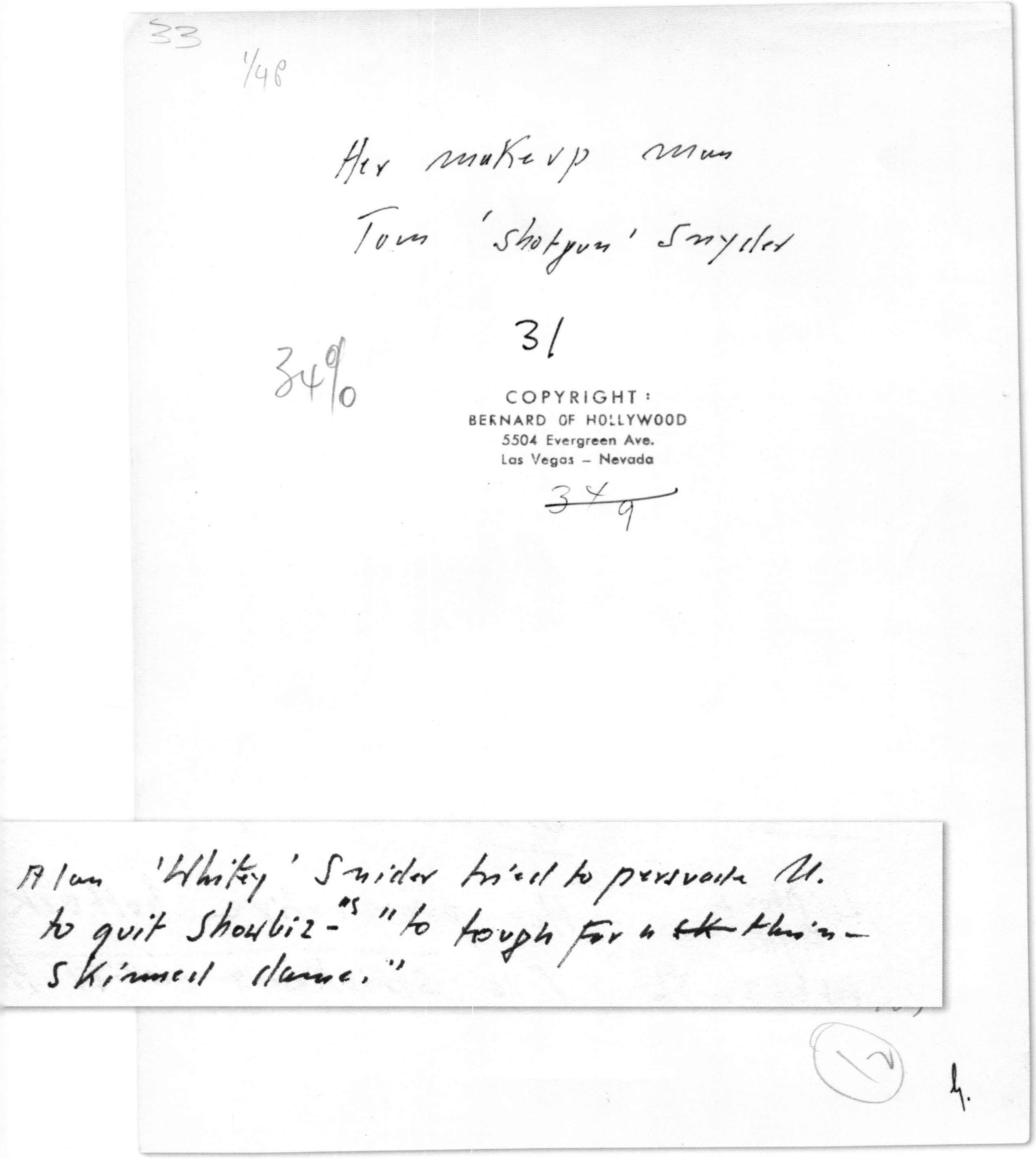

Her makeup man
Tom 'shotgun' Snyder

33
1/48

34%

31

COPYRIGHT:
BERNARD OF HOLLYWOOD
5504 Evergreen Ave.
Las Vegas — Nevada

34q

Alan 'Whitey' Snider tried to persuade M.
to quit Showbiz — "s" "to tough for a thin-
skinned dame."

Above: Reverse side of photo with Bruno Bernard's notes and photo agency stamps;
Bruno Bernard's note.

Opposite: Marilyn with friend and makeup artist Allen "Whitey" Snyder, 1954.
Acting coach Natasha Lytess hovers in the background.

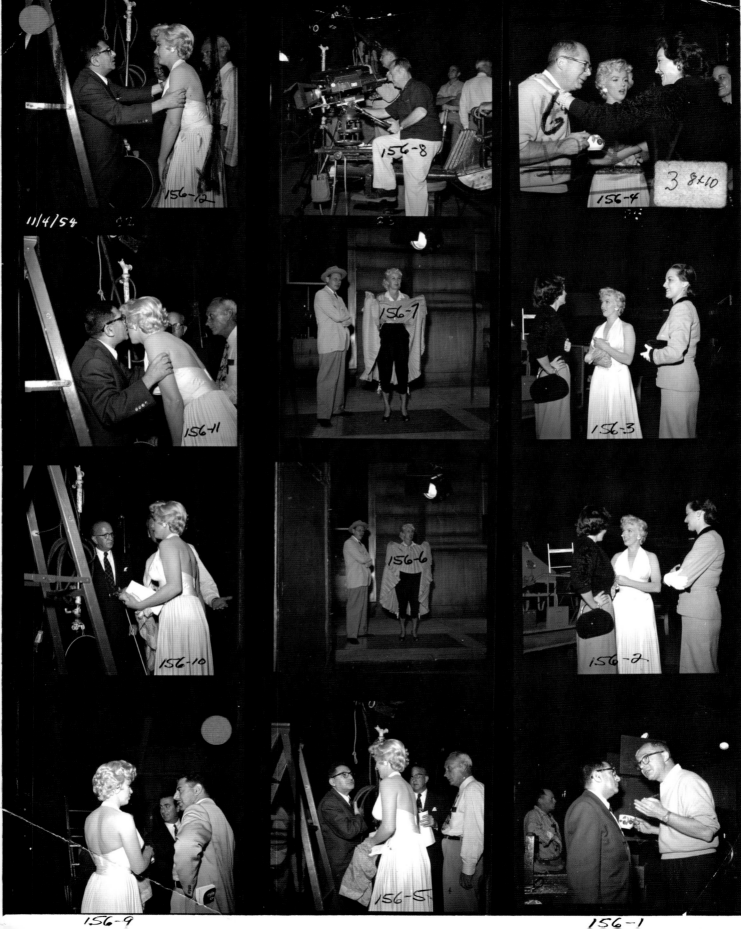

"Sid Skolsky was gushing with compliments about Marilyn's performance."

BRUNO BERNARD

Opposite: Original contact sheet; upper left corner, Sidney Skolsky and Marilyn; upper right corner,
Billy Wilder, Marilyn and Kathryn Grayson on the Hollywood set of *The Seven Year Itch,* 1954.

Above: Columnist Sidney Skolsky congratulating Marilyn on the last day of shooting; Marilyn and
photographer Sam Shaw on the Hollywood set of *The Seven Year Itch,* 1954.

The series of completely candid photos I was able to shoot on the last days on the Hollywood set of *The Seven Year Itch* shows better than any wordy essay the split personality of Norma Jean/Marilyn.

She was the vibrant Marilyn her public knew. The lost waif I had photographed a few days before was buried again under the regular doses of sleeping pills from the studio physician.

BRUNO BERNARD

"My fans want me glamorous. I won't let them down."

MARILYN MONROE

Marilyn in dressing room with set crew members, 1954.

THE LAST CONVERSATION 1956

Marilyn didn't just leave Hollywood. Such a decision required reinvention. She disappeared under dark glasses and a kerchief, and prayed not to be found. With guts, she vanished to New York, sat in Lee Strasberg's Actor's Studio where the ambiance was hard-core, took a risk, broke her Fox contract, demanded more money, approval of directors, better scripts, more respect, chose to star opposite the most distinguished actor, Sir Lawrence Olivier, and marry Pulitzer Prize winning playwright Arthur Miller. Marilyn won her war with Hollywood and then battled her own demons.

Journal '56 London: "Bernie, sorry to call you so early . . . you've known me longer than anybody in London . . . can you imagine Professor Reinhardt telling any of his actresses, 'Be sexy . . . That is what this English Sir Olivier just told me, of all people, in front of the entire crew! That's the same as if he would tell the Pope, 'be pious.'"

"But, Marilyn," I tried to get a word in edgewise, "he probably meant . . ."

"What do you mean 'probably meant'?" she shouted almost hysterically into the telephone. "Either you're sexy, or you're not, you can't fake it. It has to be spontaneous and natural or it becomes a caricature. Do you understand me, can you hear me?"

"I can hear you all right," I consoled calmly, realizing her aggressive state of anxiety was out of control. "And I understand you, as far as I can appraise the situation thousands of miles away. Perhaps it's a misunderstanding. He might have just been teasing you, the world's most famous sex symbol, advising you to throw away the lines—like Reinhardt sometimes does—to offset your obvious body language. Remember my directions in our first study sitting: 'Put sweet on hot.' After all, this great director must know what he's doing. Besides, he is a man and can feel and see that you're oozing sex from every pore of your body."

"Oh, you're all alike," she lamented, a bit of hurt innocence in her tone, "You mistake me for the characters I portray on the screen. I feel that this theatrical nobleman is plain arrogant and wanted to ridicule me, so I will eat out of his hand like the English actors who think he's God . . . Just because you resemble him enough to play his double," she teased, "doesn't mean you get to take his side."

Left: Self-portrait of Bruno Bernard, 1944.
Right: Marilyn and co-star Sir Lawrence Olivier, London press conference for *The Prince and the Showgirl*, 1957.

"Marilyn was quite wonderful, the best of all."

LAWRENCE OLIVIER, 1982

CHAPTER 6

REQUIEM 1962-2012

Reading Dad's journals and piles of notes in disarray, from the first day he met the promising teenage Norma Jean, to the endless paragraphs on her emotional demise was bitter sweet. Untangling his investigation into the sensationalism embracing her passing was a challenge.

I learned that those who really knew her, such as Pat Newcomb, her long-time publicist and confidante, were astonished when, thirteen years later, a book was published written by a man unknown to those close to Marilyn. He claimed to have married her and accused the CIA, the FBI, and Jack and Bobby Kennedy of executing her murder in order to prevent Marilyn from revealing state secrets. She supposedly had showed him a red diary naming all the "boogie men." This man, whom I personally refuse to name and thereby dignify his importance, did not possess any of the charisma of a Joe DiMaggio or an Arthur Miller.

Left: Marilyn and her husband, Arthur Miller. Manhattan, New York, 1956.
Right: Marilyn and her husband, Joe DiMaggio. Manhattan, New York, 1954.

"I was never used to being happy, so that wasn't something I ever took for granted. I did sort of think, you know, marriage did that. You see, I was brought up differently from the average American child because the average child is brought up expecting to be happy—that's it, successful, happy, and on time. Yet because of fame I was able to meet and marry two of the nicest men I'd ever met up to that time."

BRUNO BERNARD

> Marilyn Monroe was not that lucky, if one can describe the rescue from the abyss with that ambivalent word. She became Coroner's case # 81128 in the Los Angeles County Morgue. For two days nobody claimed the corpse which scant 48 hours ago was the most admired and the most often photographed body in the world.

I discovered this bittersweet photograph—Marilyn and Joe looking happy together on a fishing trip just months prior to her death, holding hands, walking along the shore of a beach near Sarasota, Florida—and I couldn't help wondering whether there was a chance of real happiness for Marilyn if she and Joe had remained together. Had timing once failed them and were they rekindling their love?

A week before her passing, Marilyn visited Cal Neva, a resort in Lake Tahoe part-owned by Frank Sinatra. A bellman told a guest that he had seen her at dawn by the pool and that on this particular day, she had come to the pool at six in the morning and he was afraid she was going to fall in. He started to head toward her when suddenly he noticed she wasn't looking at the water, but toward this hill. He followed her gaze and standing there on top of the hill was Joe DiMaggio. They stared at one another for the longest time, neither one moving, and then she turned and went back to the cottage.

My intuition was right. Morris Engelberg, Joe DiMaggio's confidant and attorney, revealed to me that Joe and Marilyn were set to remarry on August 8, 1962—the exact day she was buried. Joe told Morris, "Instead of kissing Marilyn at the altar, I kissed her in her casket."

AP Photo

Above: Bruno Bernard's note.

Below: Marilyn and Joe DiMaggio, Sarasota, Florida, 1961.

FINAL ★★★★

DAILY NEWS

NEW YORK'S PICTURE NEWSPAPER ®

5¢

Vol. 44. No. 37   Copr. 1962 News Syndicate Co. Inc.   New York 17, N.Y., Tuesday, August 7, 1962*   WEATHER: Cloudy, warm and humid.

DIMAG CLAIMS MARILYN'S BODY

Joins Star's Sister; Rites Set

Sought Herself —Then Death?

Of the many faces of Marilyn Monroe, this is perhaps the one with which her millions of admirers were least familiar. It reveals a pensive, introspective woman who was perhaps her own worst enemy. Another great enemy, according to director John Huston, was sleeplessness. As far back as 1960, he said, she was caught up in a "vicious circle" of sedatives and stimulants which, he felt, doomed her to death or an institution. Whatever the cause of her death, she is gone. Her second husband, Joe DiMaggio, who was to become one of her best friends, helped plan her funeral and burial tomorrow. Last services will be held at the mortuary of Westwood Village Me-

It was on a Saturday 20 years ago that a deeply depressed, lonely young woman still left silently the noisy revolving stage called life.

Joshua Miller

"It had to happen. I didn't know when or how, but it was inevitable."

ARTHUR MILLER

Opposite: Times Square, New York, ticker tape announcement: "Marilyn Monroe – Long Troubled . . ." 1962.

Above: Bruno Bernard at Marilyn's crypt in Westwood, California, taken by his 14-year-old grandson, Joshua Miller, two months prior to Bruno's own death in 1987.

When I was writing an article on Marilyn, I called
Pat Newcomb from Munich to authenticate something
about Mystery Man Slatzer, about whom I knew nothing
in all the years I had known Marilyn. Pat, after all,
was not only Marilyn's press spokesperson but also her
personal confidante during the last years and therefore
would be in a position to throw some light on Slatzer's
rumors. Here is the gist of my trans-Atlantic telephone
call with Pat, who at the time was working for a
New York public relations firm:

> Bruno: Hello, Pat, this is Bruno Bernard.
> You might remember me under my
> professional name, Bernard of
> Hollywood.

> Pat: I sure do. We all were sad when
> you left Hollywood. What can I
> do for you?

> Bruno: I'm presently working as a foreign
> correspondent and photo-journalist
> in Munich. The mass circulation
> magazine Quick has given me an
> assignment for a story on Marilyn.
> In this connection, you are the
> only person I know who can authen-
> ticate or refute some pertinent
> facts.

> Pat: Shoot!

> Bruno: Do you know a man by the name of
> Robert E. Slatzer?

> Pat: No, I don't.

181

Bruno: He claims that he has been a lifelong
         friend of Marilyn and was actually
         married to her for a short time.

Pat: I never heard of him.

Bruno: I didn't either. In his book he
         introduces himself as a journalist
         and a Hollywood producer who has
         devoted quite a few years to unravel-
         ling some mysteries in connection
         with Marilyn's death. He comes up
         with some allegations that sound
         utterly incredible to me.

Pat: Such as?

Bruno: Describing the police investigation
         and the coroner's report as a coverup
         for a murder plot involving the late
         attorney general and the FBI ...

         (A stony silence greeted my last remark.
         After a couple of minutes I thought
         maybe the trans-Atlantic operator had
         interrupted us, so I asked ...)

         Pat, are you still there? Did you
         hear me?

Pat: (Another long pause, then in a tough
         voice) Bruno, if I hadn't known you
         for such a long time, I would have
         hung up long ago listening to that
         trash!

         (She banged down her receiver with
         a discernible thud.)

The tone of Pat's voice and her curt reply still keep

ringing in my ears.

91

with Pat Newcomb, Marilyn's private publicist and confidante, one of the two
persons, who had seen Marilyn alive
on the last day before her death. Pat was working at the
time for a big New York advertising firm.
I had known her met her professionally years ago, when
she was one the staff of the Arthur
Jacobs publicity office. This here is the
gist of our telephone conversation.

. . . As to the proposed diary of Marilyn allegedly containing among other entries highly confidential state secrets—I stick to the old Eagle principle, "What has not been produced in court, does not exist." As long as there's no living soul who has seen Marilyn in bed with either of the Kennedys and can produce documentary evidence of such an occurrence, all surmises on these alleged affairs would be dismissed as hearsay or pure speculation by any court in the world. The legal maxim "in dubio pro reo" (the accused is presumed innocent until proven guilty), which in all civilized nations protects every private individual, does not seem to extend to a public person."

BRUNO BERNARD

The unknown man's accusations would not have caused such a great commotion had the esteemed man-of-letters, Norman Mailer, not developed a fascination with the man's creative scenarios, which spurred Mailer's imagination. When a panel discussion took place to publicize Mailer's book *Marilyn* in which Mailer speculates on her life and various fantasized scenarios of her passing, the incisive interviewer Mike Wallace asked Mailer point-blank if he believed the Kennedys had something to do with her death. Also on the panel was Enice Murray, Marilyn's housekeeper, who lived with her and was there the night she died.

MAILER: All of Hollywood was gossiping about an affair Marilyn was having with Bobby that I for one believe she was not having, although they were dear and close friends. There were all these people around in those days in the CIA and the FBI who hated the Kennedys as few Presidents have ever been hated. Some of these men thought it would not be the worst thing in the world to knock off Marilyn.

WALLACE: You don't believe that Marilyn was murdered really?

MAILER: I don't know it. I didn't know her . . .

WALLACE: I said you don't believe it . . .

MAILER: If you ask me I'd give you a handicapper estimate. I'd say it was ten to one that it was an accidental suicide. Ten to one, any way. But I could not ignore the possibility of a murder . . .

Mailer admitted in the discussion to never having interviewed Eunice Murray in his research for the book.

WALLACE: In doing research for the book Mailer never got to you.

MURRAY: I think I was reported as being in hiding.

WALLACE: That's right.

MURRAY: (laughs out loud) That's funny, my name has been in the phone book all the time. I've never tried to hide.

Mailer admitted he hated telephone interviews and that the publisher's deadline didn't allow him time for a trip to California.

Mailer coined the term "biographical novel" and *Time* labeled Mailer's book more accurately a "biographoid."

Next came the highly publicized book and BBC documentary, written and produced 26 years after her passing, based on the "unknown" man's book, Mailer's artistic license and the mysterious red diary that never materialized.

For the BBC documentary, Peter Lawford's ex-wife, who had been married to the actor for only a few weeks, traveled from Hollywood to Australia almost 10 years after their divorce to expose her former husband while he was near death in a hospital. She said that Lawford was at Marilyn's house that night to "cover up the dirty work and take care of everything."

Dad had run into Lawford at his dentist's office in Palm Springs. He had known him for years and they decided he would take Lawford's portrait the next morning.

Eunice Murray: believes it was an accident —

Robert Lipman. psychiatrist, M.M. had a chronic ongoing sleep problem. — Those people often take an overdose of sleeping pills, — ordinarily take some extra pills

"Listen, Bernie, I'm in your corner. Believe me, I wish I could be more specific "Peter Lawford's eyes got moist when he said in a whisper, "I will regret to the day I die that I didn't rush over when Marilyn called me on the phone in distress, but I listened to my agent." He was breathing heavily, his eyes were downward cast when he concluded, "You've been around too long to believe all the cock and bull stories the fast buck artists make up on us . . . ."

BRUNO BERNARD

Bruno Bernard's note.

In one of the documentary's fantastic scenarios, the "bad guys," meaning the Kennedys and their brother-in-law Peter Lawford, carted off the comatose Marilyn in an ambulance that brought her to Santa Monica hospital where she died. Even more remarkable was the allegation that Marilyn's body was slipped out of the hospital and put back in her bedroom, unbeknownst to her housekeeper Eunice Murray, in order to cover up a "political disaster."

The emergency care supervisor Van Johnson of the Santa Monica hospital told Dad, "Someone who is DOA can only be immediately released by his or her private doctor." Dad then asked what would happen in the event of a drug overdose, and he clearly stated, "It would be a coroner case and would take a couple of days."

The phonies, gossipmongers, and tearful admirers, who never knew her, rewrote history. As Senator Robert Kennedy's lawyer, John Bates, voiced publicly on the BBC documentary, "I would like to cross-examine them. I think they are lying."

John Bates wrote a three-page letter to Dad, dated October 8, 1986, proving that he and his family were with Robert Kennedy, Kennedy's wife Ethel, and their two children, at his ranch in Gilroy, 300 miles east of Los Angeles on August 4 and 5, 1962. Therefore, "It would have been impossible for Robert Kennedy to be in Los Angeles on the 4th unless he had a twin." As evidence, Bates sent snapshots of Senator Kennedy and his family that were taken that weekend, outlining the exact time and place of each shot and proving that it was impossible for Senator Kennedy to have been in Los Angeles the day or night of Marilyn's death.

Searching through Dad's files and suitcases, I couldn't locate any of the photographs that were mentioned in John Bates' letter. They had disappeared, along with the truth. I managed to locate John Bates' son, John, and urged him to search for the photos, telling him, "Our fathers fought for justice and truth, and we must carry out their honorable intentions." I also repeated his father's words:

> "In memory of Robert Kennedy, at least Ethel and Robert's children deserve that the truth be told and that Robert's memory be cleared of all these falsehoods about where he was at the time Marilyn died."
>
> —John Bates

Two weeks later, fifteen photos were in my hands. John's younger brother, Charles, had written back. "I went down to Janaca to oversee the harvesting, I picked up the scrap book that had the Kennedy pictures."

Certainly there have been moments when I doubted Dad's obsession with polishing the tarnished legacies of Marilyn and the Kennedys. "Since the main protagonists of this real life drama are all dead, it is up to us living to come to the defense of these personalities who cannot defend themselves." Dad had fled Nazi Germany to the land of the free and wanted to hold onto his belief in Camelot and not see the Kennedy era go down as "Sodom and Gomorrah." He longed for the Kennedys to go down in history as the founders of the Peace Corps, as courageous fighters for social justice, and as the inaugurators of the Good Neighbor Policy and the peaceful existence with Russia—and for Bobby to be remembered for his fearless efforts to destroy the Mafia—rather than merely as womanizers implicated in the murder of Marilyn Monroe, his close friend.

JOHN B. BATES, JR.

October 31, 2010

Dear Susan,

Here's the DVD with the photos from the Kennedy visit and some correspondence from my father. There are other letters attached to the e-mail from my brother that I forwarded to you.

Ethel, Bobby and their four oldest kids were there (Kathleen, Joe, Bobby, and David). In the photos, I'm the one with the football.

Hope this helps.

John

Above: Letter from John Bates Jr. to Susan Bernard, 2010.

Opposite: Letter from John Bates to Bruno Bernard, 1986.

John B Bates
225 Bush Street
San Francisco
California 94104

October 8, 1986

Dr Bruno Bernard
C/o Haus Maria
Höckstrafse 14
8170 Bad Tölz BRD
West Germany

Dear Dr Bernard

Finally, I found some time to respond to your letter and the various telephone calls that I have received from your daughter, Susan Bernard.

In the early nineteen forties and during the war years, Jack Kennedy and I became relatively good friends. Paul 'Red' Fay, Kennedy and I were all in the Navy and in the Pacific Fleet. Red was a close personal friend of both Jack and me and he made an effort to bring us together. When Jack became President, he asked me to join Bob Kennedy in the Attorney General's office, but I, most reluctantly, declined.

In 1962, when the American Bar Convention was planned for San Francisco, I called Bob and asked him if he would like to come out and spend some time with us at our ranch in Gilroy before the Convention.

". . . Since the main protagonists of this real life drama are all dead, it is up to us living to come to the defense of these personalities who cannot defend themselves."

BRUNO BERNARD

he addressed the American Bar Association on Monday morning at the Fairmont Hotel in San Francisco.

There was no way that Bob could have left our ranch at any time that weekend, gone to Santa Monica and returned to the ranch. Even if he had attempted such an impossible feat, we certainly would have known about it. The ranch is located in the hills and there is very little flat land. That is the reason for the long trek up to the top of the ranch Saturday afternoon where there is a flat where we played touch football. This field is now known as Kennedy flat.

It would be very difficult for a helicopter to land at the ranch and, particularly so, without anybody knowing about it. The dogs would have gone berserk and wakened everybody. It would have taken much planning and considerable time for the then Attorney General to the picked up by helicopter, taken to Santa Monica and then brought back to the ranch during the middle of the night. The ranch is not easy to find. As a matter of fact, the FBI agent got lost in the process of trying to deliver the Kennedy luggage. It is necessary to open and close two gates to get in and out of the ranch and it is at least an hours drive to the nearest commercial airport which is in San José.

Those purported eyewitnesses who claim to have seen Bob Kennedy in southern California on Saturday are either lying, victims of hallucinations, or they have been victimised by falsely crafted theories.

Very truly yours,

I have chosen the most pertinent photographic evidence to illustrate the letter John Bates wrote to my dad in October 1986. I've excluded some of the photos in which Robert Kennedy was not present, as they are not relevant.

Picture No 1 is of Bob and our foreman, Roland Snyder, taken on Saturday morning while we were saddling up for our ride. Picture No 3 is of me, Bob, Kathleen, Ethel and Nancy as we were ready to take off. Picture No 4 is at the site of the Miller home where we met Roland who had driven up with those who had not been riding horses. The ride took more than three hours of the morning. After returning, there was swimming and lunch around the Pool (pictures 6 and 8).

After lunch and at the urging of Bob Kennedy, we embarked on a hike to the top of the ranch where we played touch football. It is about a two-mile hike, almost entirely uphill and the entire expedition was done on foot. Picture 13 was taken near the top of the ranch. Picture 14 shows Bob at the site where we played touch football and picture 15 was taken by me in the middle of the game.

That evening when the children came dressed to dinner, Bob threw them all into the swimming pool (picture 18), so they had to go back to their rooms, dry off and get dressed all over again. Nancy insisted that the children eat first, which they did; and Ethel sat us down together for dinner at about 8:15 pm. Needless to say, all of us were tired and retired to our rooms for the night, Bob was working on the speech that he gave to the American Bar Association Convention in San Francisco on Monday morning after the weekend.

On Sunday morning . . . I drove the Kennedys to San Francisco and, specifically, to the Paul Fay, Senior's apartment. Picture 19 shows us getting ready to leave."

The occasion was the unveiling of the bust of the late President John Fitzgerald Kennedy at the Catholic University in Rio de Janeiro. I approached the senator and said, "Senator, I believe that I am the only press corps member present that had the privilege of photographing the President when he made his speech 'Ich bin ein Berliner' in front of Schonberg City Hall in Berlin. As a Native Berliner who had to flee his homeland because of the Nazis, I got goose pimples when the tens of thousands of your listeners were galvanized into frenetic applause. This scene and the torchlight parade of the Berlin students to Schöenberg City Hall at the news of the President's death flashed back into my mind throughout your speech today."

I could hardly finish my sentence because I was so emotionally charged. Robert Kennedy with the reputation of a tough Irish street fighter had moist eyes and pressed my hand warmly.

Commentating in a low voice he said, "I'll never forget that scene as long as I live. The torchlight parade by the students was the most touching tribute to the late President. I am happy that you were able to be present at the lasting memorial for him and what he stood for."

This totally unexpected human rapport made me tongue-tied. I felt in a grip of rendezvous with destiny that drowned out all questions of a personal nature about Marilyn at such an historical moment.

BRUNO BERNARD

Above: Bruno Bernard's note.

Opposite above: Original proof sheet of Senator Robert Kennedy in Rio de Janiero, 1965.

Opposite below: Photograph of Senator Robert Kennedy in Rio de Janiero when Bruno Bernard presented him with a photograph of his brother, John Kennedy, 1965.

MARILYN MONROE — quote on age

"I like old people; they have great qualities younger people don't have. I want to grow old without face lifts. They take the life out of a face, the character. I want to have the courage to be loyal to the face I've made. Sometimes I think it would be easier to avoid old age, to die young, but then you'd never complete your life, would you? You'd never wholly know yourself."

Poor Marilyn. She never got to wholly know herself — or to grow old. —

— Her contacts with an old sage, the ~~Scholarly~~ poet & Scholarly biographer of Lincoln, Carl Sandburg, was a love at first sight encounter. He ~~pub~~ posthumously published her poem —

LIFE
Also cf.
Clare Boothe
Luce in 'Life'

Opposite: Bruno Bernard's note.

Above: "Norma Jean Killed Marilyn," proposed book cover designed by Bruno Bernard, 1986.

For millions of men all over the world, she was the most desirable love object, and yet she died at a young age, lonely and desperate because she was unable to form a permanent union of mutual love and respect with one private individual.

All the evidence points to the fact that Marilyn did not want to commit suicide. Marilyn died during the night between the August 4 and 5, 1962. Her death was an accident due to a lethal blend of an overdose of Nembutal sleeping pills and alcohol. This does not rule out, however, the correct analysis that she had committed suicide over the years on the installment plan.

As many as three times during her marriage to Arthur Miller she had attempted to do away with herself, only to be saved at the last minute by her alert and concerned husband. Her frantic telephone SOS calls during her last night seem to indicate she was seeking help. However, with the exception of Peter Lawford none of her close friends were reachable. The universally worshipped love goddess died a lonely human creature on her bed with the telephone receiver still in her hand.

BRUNO BERNARD

Will we ever know what happened the night of August 5th, 1962.

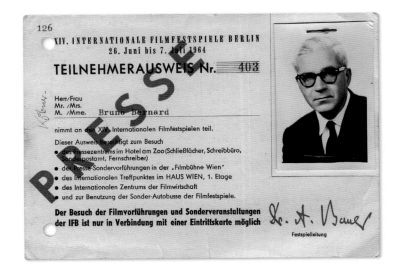

LEGACY

By the early 60s, Dad had sold his three landmark studios to return to his homeland, Berlin, and become a foreign photojournalist, covering the Eichmann trial for *Der Spiegel*. He was so moved by the proceedings that he compiled the bestseller *Israel Impressions*. In '69, he began building a Mediterranean three-story villa on the pristine beaches of Palma de Mallorca, Spain, and plunged into his own artistic evolution and intellectual discovery. At the entrance was the sign "Casa Bernard," and at the bottom of a long, pebbled stairway, he paid homage to Marilyn, building an enchanted rock garden and—christening it "Norma Jean."

I am certain that when, in 1946, the teenage Norma Jean Dougherty wiggled aimlessly past my father on Sunset Boulevard and he gave her his card, he could not have imagined that over a half-century later I would be carrying on his legacy, preserving, exhibiting, and publishing his legendary photographs of Norma Jean and winning legal battles to protect both his and her photographic rights. He would have been amazed at the unheard-of sums that vintage prints of her with his signature on the reverse sell for, at the rush of new books, calendars, and apparel that his fame would give rise to. He would be awed by the appearance of

her image and his famous Bernard of Hollywood signature on a crystal iPhone cover; on satin intimate wear with pretty bows; high-tech wall graphics that stick to glass; high-end cushy leather wallets, keychains, evening bags and cowboy boots; Italian schoolgirl notepads, satchels and binders; T-shirts beautifully glittered; T-shirts altering her with edgy tattoos; bomber jackets, Marilyn swinging inside sea blue, rose and silver Christmas ornaments; her face on collectible coins secured in vaults, salt and pepper shakers and sleep masks; her flying skirt scene recreated in a glass snow globe. The good sport Marilyn on martini and shot glasses, exquisite Italian china tea and espresso sets; life-size stand-ups that greet me at airports; motorcycle decals and biker bandanas. Her body in pieces waiting to be put together in a glossy jigsaw puzzle; teenagers, mature women and drag queens bang on my door begging for candy in Bernard of Hollywood-inspired Marilyn white dresses and platinum wigs on Halloween.

My dad undoubtedly would have been proud that his grandson, my son Joshua Miller, would at only 23 write a critically acclaimed novel, *The Mao Game,* whose central character, a famous Hollywood glamour photographer, would be inspired by him.

Above: Bruno Bernard's foreign press credentials, 1966.

Opposite: Bruno and Marilyn, 1953.

There are more books written about Marilyn than about heads of state. On runways from Paris to Hong Kong, her distinct style is mirrored. Today's young Hollywood places her on the goddess pedestal and emulates her unattainable essence. Fifty years after her passing, Hollywood scrambles to write screenplays about her with a new angle, a fresh approach. Stars are under pressure because everyone has their own idea of who she was. In this rush of Marilyn madness, studios race to release their film first. Each is convinced their movie has the most bite—even if the story is told from the vantage point of Marilyn's dog.

The girl who was never convinced of her true last name would be astonished. Today, in hundreds of countries, her fabricated movie name is copyrighted, branded and protected by those who claim ownership and those who have convinced themselves it's theirs. Photographers mortgage houses to claim her image, others pay off politicians to change the law. Her famous signature is priceless—be it found on a check, a grocery list, or instructions to her gardener. Graphic designers alter it, forgers trace it, and handwriting experts are consulted. She creates employment and cash flow in a bad economy. Step up to the wheel, spin, get lucky, make a pact with Marilyn and your destiny can be altered.

Being a thread weaving its way through the Marilyn mythology has been an astonishing journey with no regrets. Thanks, Dad.

Susan Bernard, 1954.

In a spiritual way Marilyn is more alive today than when she was alive. The German poet Theodor Fontane wrote: one dies twice, the second time is oblivion. ~~This second death~~ In this sense Marilyn will live forever,

AUTHOR SUSAN BERNARD

Susan Bernard is the author of six books, including the best-selling *Bernard of Hollywood's Ultimate Pin-Up Book* and *Joyous Motherhood*. Founder and President of Bernard of Hollywood Publishing/Renaissance Road, Inc., she preserves and internationally exhibits, publishes and licenses her late father's work. Susan has a cult following, having starred at the age of 16 in *Faster, Pussycat, Kill! Kill!* and co-starred with such legends as Orson Welles and Henry Fonda. For the networks, she developed the docudramas "The Diary of Anais Nin," "The Nellie Bly Story" and "The Ernie Davis Story." With Whoopi Goldberg, Susan co-produced the feature film *The Mao Game*, based on her son Joshua Miller's first novel. A resident of Los Angeles' Hancock Park, she is an active member of PEN USA and is currently working on a novel.

Above left: Susan Bernard, 2011.

Above right: In 1984, the Academy of Motion Picture Arts and Sciences honored Bruno Bernard. Seen here with his daughter, Susan Bernard, and his grandson, Joshua Miller.

Below: Bruno Bernard photographing Susan, at the villa in Palma de Mallorca, 1971.

Acknowledgements

The process of this book has been a collaboration of passion, raw nerves and sheer hard work. I want to thank especially my multitalented right hand Patricia Campbell, who was relentless getting the job done; my innovative designer Maria Grillo who went beyond the call of duty to make the book all it has become, and along with her associate Jason Harvey implemented and supported my vision; my creative director at Bernard of Hollywood for over a decade, David Wills, for his expertise and encouragement; my agent and production manager on this project, the determined Gary Chassman, who made it all possible by running a tight ship; and my long-time legal guardian angel Arthur Stashower, whose assistance is immeasurable.

I want to thank the driving force at Sterling Publishing, the insightful Michael Fragnito, who stepped up; my executive editor Barbara Berger, who believed that a pictorial book could be gorgeous, cool and edgy; and to my editor Laura Swerdloff, who took the book to the level it deserved.

My son Joshua Miller, the genius, and Mark Fortin raise the bar on artistic integrity and are my sounding board amidst the chaos. Their love makes all the difference.

The legendary Jane Russell, for contributing so much; Lindsay Lohan, for sharing her very personal thoughts; Jason Weinberg and Evan Hainey at Untitled Entertainment; John Bates Jr. and Charles Bates, who without hesitation, honored both our father's mission to defend the deceased who cannot defend themselves; and Joe DiMaggio's trusted friend and counsel Morris Englebert.

Many have contributed to my dreams and the Bernard of Hollywood story that inspired this volume. I'd like to thank in alphabetical order: The Academy of Motion Picture Arts and Sciences, Russell Adams, Vin Alabiso of *The New York Times* Store, Wes Andrews, Suzie Ariel, Authentic Brands Group: James Salter, Perry Wolfman, Joel Weinshanker, Jordan Goodman, Terri L. DiPaolo and Paul Cohen, Lois Banner, Bonnie Bauman, Celeste Bendele, Karen Black, Ruth Bernard Brande, Kate Braverman, George Brich, Dolley Carlson, Frank Caruso of King Features, Sylvia Cohen, Sheryl Conaway, Steve Conaway, Mariana Diamos, Mina Dobic, Simon Doonan, Jim Fitzgerald, Rory Flynn, Biond Fury, Clark Gable, Sandy Gellhorn, Marilyn Goldberg of Museum Masters, Ita Golzman of King Features, Kim Goodwin, Joshua Greene, Hugh Hefner, Alan Hipwell, Dr. Tom Horowitz, Cathy Horyn of *The New York Times*, Hilary Katersky, Milton Katselas, Tom Kelley Jr., Carole Kismaric, Alana Lambrose, Piper Laurie, Michael Lou of VIP Entertainment, Melonie Magruder, Leas Marie, Chandanni Miglino, Jason Miller, Marilyn Monroe, Michael Morris, the Museum of Modern Art, New York, Pat Newcomb, Julie Newmar, Anaïs Nin, PEN USA, Peter Poon, Tyrone Power, Lee Purcell, James Ragan, Mary Rakow, Max Reinhardt, Rachel Resnick, Roger Richman, Aishah Roberts, Gwen Roberts, Ginger Rogers, Peter Rosenblatt, Mark Rosner of CMG, Neal Roth, Susie Roth, Diane Sawyer, Aaron Schmulewitz, Cheney Shapiro, Melissa Shaw, Maria Shriver, Sharon Sindell, Lili St. Cyr, Edwige Saint-Jacques, Naomi Sommerfeld, Etheleen Staley, Anna Strasberg, David Strasberg, Benedict Taschen, Kevin Thomas, *Vanity Fair:* Susan White and Ann Schneider, Alberto Vargas, Donald Wallens, William Morris Endeavor: Norman R. Brokaw, Chairman Emeritus, Judson Williams, Marilyn Wilson, Takouhy Wise, Walter Yetnikoff, and George Zeno.

Bibliography

"The Creature from the Black Lagoon: Marilyn Monroe and Whiteness." Banner, Lois W. Cinema Journal Volume 47. No. 4, Summer 2008.

Marilyn Monroe und die Kamera, Baseda-Maass, Karin. Munich: Schirmer/Mosel, 1989.

Requiem for Marilyn, Bernard, Bruno. U.K.: The Krensal Press, 1987.

"Say Goobye to the President: Marilyn and the Kennedys." prod. George Cary and Christopher Oligati. DVD. British Broadcasting Corportation, 1996. 85 mins.

Joe DiMaggio: The Hero's Life, Cramer, Richard Ben. New York: Touchstone, 2001.

DiMaggio: Setting the Record Straight, Engelberg, Morris and Marv Schneider. Minnesota: MBI Publishing Co, 2003.

"MM Remembered." Playboy Magazine. HMH Publishing Co., Inc. Chicago. January 1964: 100–109.

Marilyn Monroe: Confidential, Pepitone, Lena and William Stadiem. New York: Simon & Schuster, 1979.

Marilyn Monroe: A Life of the Actress, Rollyson, Carl E. Michigan: UMI Research Press, 1986.

Marilyn: An Untold Story, Rosten, Norman. New York: Signet, 1973.

Jane Russell: My Path & My Detours, Russell, Jane. New York: Franklin Watts, Inc, 1985.

Robert Mitchum: "baby, I don't care", Server, Lee. New York: St. Martin's Griffin, 2002.

The Marilyn Scandal, Shevey, Sandra. New York: William Morrow & Co., Inc., 1988.

On Photography, Sontag, Susan. New York: Delta Publishing Co., Inc., 1973.

Goddess: The Secret Lives of Marilyn Monroe, Summers, Anthony. New York: Onyx, 1986.

Marilyn Monroe: An Uncensored Biography, Zolotow, Maurice. New York: Bantam Books, 1960.

WILDLIFE

OF THE WORLD

WILDLIFE

OF THE WORLD

First American Edition, 2015
Published in the United States by DK Publishing
345 Hudson Street, New York, New York 10014

Copyright © 2015 Dorling Kindersley Limited
DK, a Penguin Random House Company

15 16 17 18 19 10 9 8 7 6 5 4 3 2 1

001–259136–October/2015

Published in Great Britain by Dorling Kindersley Limited.
A catalog record for this book is available from the Library of Congress
ISBN 978-1-4654-3804-1

DK books are available at special discounts when purchased in bulk for sales promotions, premiums, fund-raising, or educational use. For details, contact: DK Publishing Special Markets, 345 Hudson Street, New York, New York 10014 SpecialSales@dk.com

Printed in China

**A WORLD OF IDEAS:
SEE ALL THERE IS TO KNOW**

www.dk.com

Smithsonian

Established in 1846, the Smithsonian—the world's largest museum and research complex—includes 19 museums and galleries and the National Zoological Park. The total number of artifacts, works of art, and specimens in the Smithsonian's collections is estimated at 138 million, the bulk of which is contained in the National Museum of Natural History, which holds more than 126 million specimens and objects. The Smithsonian is a renowned research center, dedicated to public education, national service, and scholarship in the arts, sciences, and history.

Consultants

▌MAMMALS
Professor David Macdonald CBE is a leading world authority on mammals, and is founder and Director of the Wildlife Conservation Research Unit at Oxford University, UK. Aside from his many scientific publications, he is known for his prize-winning books and films, such as *Meerkats United*.

▌BIRDS
David Burnie studied Zoology at Bristol University, UK, and has contributed to nearly 150 books on animals and the environment. He is a Fellow of the Zoological Society of London.

▌REPTILES
Dr. Colin McCarthy is a scientific associate of the Life Sciences Department, and formerly Collection Manager of Reptiles, Amphibians, and Fish, at the Natural History Museum, London, UK.

▌AMPHIBIANS
Professor Tim Halliday retired as Professor of Biology at the Open University in 2009 but continues to pursue his interest in the reproductive biology of amphibians.

▌INVERTEBRATES
Dr. George C. McGavin is a zoologist, author, explorer, and television host. He is an Honorary Research Associate of the Oxford University Museum of Natural History and a Research Associate of the Department of Zoology at Oxford University, UK. His TV credits include *Expedition Borneo*, *Lost Land of the Jaguar*, *Lost Land of the Tiger*, and *Monkey Planet*.

▌GENERAL CONSULTANT
Dr. Kim Dennis-Bryan is a paleontologist who worked at the Natural History Museum, London, before becoming an associate lecturer in life and environmental sciences at the Open University, UK.

▌EDITORIAL CONSULTANT
Dr. Don E. Wilson is Curator Emeritus, Vertebrate Zoology, National Museum of Natural History, Smithsonian. He is the author of more than 250 scientific publications and 25 books on a variety of topics, including the mammals of North America, bats, humans, biodiversity, and mammal species of the world. He is an elected Fellow of the AAAS, and Honorary member of ASM.

Contributors

Jamie Ambrose is a UK-based American author, editor, and journalist with a special interest in the natural world.

Richard Beatty (glossary writer) is a writer and editor based in Edinburgh, UK.

Dr. Amy-Jane Beer is a biologist, nature writer, and editor of the UK charity PTES (People's Trust for Endangered Species) *Wildlife World* magazine.

Derek Harvey is a naturalist with particular interests in evolutionary biology, and writer for titles that include DK's *Science* and *The Natural History Book*.

Ben Hoare is features editor of *BBC Wildlife* magazine, UK.

Rob Hume is a natural history writer and editor with a lifetime interest in wildlife, especially birds. He is author of more than 20 books, including DK's *Bird*, and *Birds of Europe and North America*.

Tom Jackson is a zoologist and science writer based in Bristol, UK.

Steve Parker has a zoology degree and has written more than 200 books and websites on nature, ecology, conservation, and evolution.

Dr. Katie Parsons has a PhD in animal behavior and ecology. She is currently a freelance natural history writer and conservation consultant.

John Woodward has written more than 40 books and many hundreds of articles on all aspects of the natural world.

DK LONDON

Senior Art Editor Ina Stradins
Senior Editors Janet Mohun, Peter Frances
Project Editor Gill Pitts
US Editor Jenny Siklos
Project Art Editor Francis Wong
Designer Simon Murrell
Editorial Assistant Frankie Piscitelli
Indexer Hilary Bird
Picture Researcher Liz Moore
New Photography Gary Ombler
Cartography Simon Mumford, Ed Merritt
Jacket Designer Mark Cavanagh
Jacket Editor Claire Gell
Jacket Design Development Manager Sophia MTT
Pre-production Producer Francesca Wardell
Producer Rita Sinha
Managing Art Editor Michael Duffy
Managing Editor Angeles Gavira
Art Director Karen Self
Design Director Phil Ormerod
Publisher Liz Wheeler
Publishing Director Jonathan Metcalf

DK INDIA

Senior Art Editor Mahua Mandal
Senior Editor Vineetha Mokkil
Project Editor Dharini Ganesh
Art Editors Divya P R, Anjali Sachar
Editor Susmita Dey
Managing Art Editor Sudakshina Basu
Managing Editor Rohan Sinha
Picture Researchers Deepak Negi, Surya Sankash Sarangi
Jacket Designer Suhita Dharamjit
Managing Jackets Editor Saloni Singh
Production Manager Pankaj Sharma
Pre-production Manager Balwant Singh
Senior DTP Designers Harish Aggarwal, Vishal Bhatia
DTP Designer Vijay Kandwal

SMITHSONIAN ENTERPRISES

President Christopher A. Liedel
Senior Vice President, Consumer and Education Products Carol LeBlanc
Vice President, Consumer and Education Products Brigid Ferraro
Licensing Manager Ellen Nanney
Product Development Manager Kealy Gordon

DATA PANELS

Summary information is given at the start of each profile. Measurements are for adults of the species and may be a typical range, single-figure average, or maximum, depending on available records.

↔ LENGTH (all groups)
MAMMALS Head and body excluding tail. For dolphins, whales, seals, sea lions, manatees, and dugongs it includes the tail. **BIRDS** Tip of bill to tip of tail (except penguins, ostrich, rhea, and emu, which indicates height from feet to head). **REPTILES** Tip of snout to tip of tail (except tortoises and turtles where it is the length of the upper shell). **FISH AND AMPHIBIANS** Head and body, including tail. **INSECTS** Body length; wingspan for butterflies and moths.

⚖ WEIGHT (Mammals, birds, reptiles, amphibians, and fish only)
Body weight.

🍴 DIET All diet listed by commas (except caterpillars' diet; butterflies' diet, separated by a semicolon).

🌙 BREEDING SEASON (Amphibians only) The time of year in which breeding occurs.

✖ STATUS (all groups) *Wildlife of the World* uses the IUCN Red List (see p459) and other threat categories, as follows:
Critically endangered (IUCN) Facing an extremely high risk of extinction in the wild in the immediate future.
Endangered (IUCN) Facing a very high risk of extinction in the wild in the near future.
Vulnerable (IUCN) Facing a high risk of extinction in the wild in the medium-term future.
Near threatened (IUCN) Strong possibility of becoming endangered in the near future.
Common/Locally common (IUCN: Least concern) Low-risk category that includes widespread and common species.
Not known (IUCN: Data deficient, Not evaluated) Not a threat category. Population and distribution data is insufficient for assessment. Data not yet assessed against IUCN criteria.

🏠 HABITAT SYMBOLS

Temperate and deciduous forest, open woodland

Evergreen, coniferous, and boreal forest and woodland

Tropical forest and rainforest, dry forest of Madagascar

Mountains, highlands, scree slopes, any habitat considered alpine or subalpine conditions

Desert and semi-desert

Open habitats including grassland, moor, heath, savanna, fields, and scrub

Wetlands and all still bodies of water, including lakes, ponds, pools, marshes, bogs, and swamps

Rivers, streams, and all flowing water

Mangrove swamps, above or below the waterline

Coastal areas including beaches and cliffs, areas just above high tide, in the intertidal zone, and in shallow, offshore waters

Seas and oceans

Coral reefs and waters immediately around them

Polar regions, including tundra and icebergs

Urban areas, including buildings, parks, and gardens

LOCATION MAP

Shows distribution of species in the wild

CONTENTS

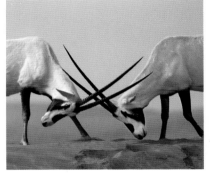

AFRICA
174

ASIA
244

AUSTRALASIA
310

ANTARCTICA
360